VERACITY

LORI TUCKER

Lori Tucker/Veracity
Printed in the United States of America

Veracity/ Lori Tucker -- 1st ed.

ISBN 9798714129957 Print Edition

For every child who lost their voice

INTRODUCTION

For years, I didn't have a voice to protect myself. For years, I knew something was missing from my life. Tragedy was a big part of my life, as it is for many of us. I have been diagnosed with PTSD, and I have spent years looking for a balance. I strive to be a normal person, but now I have the strength to ask: what is normal? Normalcy is, in many ways and for many people, just a mirage. We all have blemishes. Those blemishes make all of us unique, which is good. For me, seeking balance means being willing to share my story.

For those of you I personally know, please know that I haven't had a voice to protect myself from people who have silenced me and made self-preservation impossible. For many, many years, I felt something was missing from my life. Knowing that tragedy was a big part of my life is something that I've learned to live with, as much as it hurts me. Because of those experiences, I spent many years looking for a balance in my life, for peace. This book is my way of finding that.

Though I have researched and verified these memories with family members, this is my story, my experience. Some names or identifying details have been changed to protect the privacy of the individuals involved.

CHAPTER 1

Legend has it that my grandfather gave Dad a gun to finish us off. But I'm getting way ahead of myself.

My story begins in southern California, though I have no memory of the years I lived there. I was born in May of 1965. My father, Eugene (Gene) Price, was a redheaded Irishman. My mother, Carol May, was Latina. Not the most common bedfellows, but the combination made for some interesting and rather remarkable-looking kids. My sisters were very fair complected and took after Dad. My brother, Ted (not his real name), had dark hair and light skin and took after them both. Me? I was all Mom. Dark complexion, raven-black hair, and solid brown eyes. My parents had their own little Pocahontas if you will. They named me Lori Lawanda Price.

I don't remember those years in California, though later in my life, I often wished we had stayed there in the Golden State. Family tells me that our life was peaceful there.

My dad was offered a business opportunity in a small town forty miles outside of St. Louis, Missouri. There was a store that he could buy, a place where he and my mother could work. So off we went to Elsberry, Missouri, a town close to the banks of the Mississippi River.

We settled into a quaint little subdivision known as Lakeview with an actual lake that I remember fishing in and skipping stones on. My parents established themselves in a small store that sold bread, milk, and other essentials to the neighborhood and offered deliveries to both businesses and residents of Elsberry. True to his word, Dad was able to provide for our family.

Sometimes my dad would let me go with him on his deliveries. I sat on the truck's bench seat next to him, watching the dust motes float through the air as Petula Clark's "Downtown" played on the radio. I can remember feeling proud at age four to be included in such important business. I'd look over at his strong arms driving the truck, and he'd smile at me.

"Hi, Dad," I'd say.

"Hi, Lori. Doing OK?"

"Yep."

Those were golden days.

On deliveries, the customers would always greet me, "It's cute little Lori!" My favorite delivery to make was to the school. The lunch ladies would always give me a piece of cheese—to this day, it's still one of my favorite snacks.

Sadly, grocery-delivering, cheese-snacking Dad slowly morphed into something darker. As days were changing to nights and seasons were passing, my father started changing too . . . from a provider to a physical/mental abuser who wanted nothing more than to destroy me, my mother, and my brother and sisters. It was confusing. By day, he was a solid, steady presence. But at night, he drank heavily, and the drunker he got, the meaner he was.

After beers began, Dad shifted from the radio-playing daytime dad to a rampaging threat, stomping through the house, looking for a fight. Usually, it was my mom who shouldered the burden of Dad's rage.

My parents spent their days and some of their nights at the store. Before kindergarten, I was there too, though memories of it are vague. I can recall narrow aisles just packed with cases of canned soup and toilet paper. There was of course the candy rack, placed strategically in front of the cash register where Mom or Dad could keep an eye on it and the kids who came to linger by the Hershey's Bars and Tootsie Pops.

As soon as school got out, my sisters, Carol and Keri, came to collect me. I'd spend the afternoon hours having a snack and watching *Sesame Street* while they did homework. Being ten and eleven years older than me, my sisters were my main caregivers and protectors. They watched over Ted too, who is three years older than me.

Most of my early memories are from that Lakeview house. I can recall the wood paneling in the living room, sticky from the smoker's smog. By dinner most nights, the air was heavy with tar and smoke from my parents' cigarettes, and there was a funk from my father's 12-pack-a-night habit that soured the air . . . as did the anger that simmered until it boiled over every evening. A normal night in the Price household included hearing my parents yell and bicker continuously. It was almost on a loop.

"Did you bring home any bread?"

"Stop nagging me, woman!"

Mom really tried to keep the peace, but some nights it was a lost cause. Saying the sky was blue would have started an argument. When that happened, we kids would make ourselves scarce while the level of the yelling got louder and louder. My dad grew more and more angry and more and more drunk until he would hit my mother.

Still small and terrified, I did what my sisters told me to do. I hid. Beneath the bed sometimes, but mostly in the closet under piles of blankets, there I sat, wide-eyed and terrified.

There was an orphanage in St. Louis on Fee Fee Road that Dad would sometimes threaten to send me to. When not punching my mother or sisters, he'd thunder on, "Where's Lori?!?! Tonight we're going to the orphanage!"

"Where is she!?" he would thunder, and I'd hope the blankets were a strong enough fortress to keep me safe.

Mom stayed with Dad for years, frightened to try and make it on her own with four kids.

One particular night stands out in my memory. The yelling and smacking sounds of hands on skin crescendoed to a level I hadn't heard before. Then, amidst the slurred hollering about Mom and us and the store, I heard the word "gun."

My sisters reacted quickly to this new threat. "Hide, Lori! Hide like you've never hidden before!" To the back of the closet I went, under some laundry, where I heard only my father's angry voice . . . then a click. More growling from Dad, followed by another click. I was too young then to understand, but later figured out that Dad had retrieved his inheritance and was "playing" Russian Roulette with Mom as he pointed the revolver at her head. One bullet in the chamber, ready to blow her head off at any minute.

Even now, telling this story as an adult, the same feeling of terror returns to me. More than once, I spent an evening in that closet with my heart in my stomach, my bottom lip quivering, my eyes wide open with a fear no child should ever experience. I would only come out when my sisters would tell me it was safe. My father had either passed out or left.

The trauma of terror doesn't ever really leave your body, even if you know logically the danger is over. I'm a grown woman with gray hairs, and I can still feel that pit in my preschooler's stomach, that tingle of electricity running to my fingertips and toes. Fear lingers.

As I look back now, the closet is probably the first place someone would look for a small child, but not Dad, which should give you an idea of how drunk he would get.

CHAPTER 2

We kids continued surviving in the house, trying not to poke the bear. I can't remember a lot about those times; I was five, after all. Carol tells me that one time I was getting into Dad's cigarettes and he threw me against the wall. I wasn't injured. I do remember the time Dad punched Carol in the face and broke her jaw. Since she was my main caregiver, I remember being very scared and angry that she'd been hurt. Carol Jean looks just like Dad, yet they couldn't be more different.

One person who consistently avoided physical punishment from Dad was Ted. Dad absolutely adored my brother. The two of them would play baseball in the yard and joke and laugh together. On the nights Dad was drunk and violent, Ted was never in the line of fire. I don't remember where he was, but it wasn't in the closet with me. And Ted was never threatened with the orphanage in St. Louis.

It's hard to think back on those times. From the vantage point of an adult, I can see now that we needed help. There was a problem in our house but getting help would have required that we first acknowledge the problem. All of us knew on some level that we shouldn't have to live in fear of violence from a family member. Yet, no one could talk about it. There simply was no model for that in our family.

Mom was a sweep-things-under-the-rug kind of person. That mode of operating would thread through her entire life.

But it turned out that just because Mom wasn't talking about Dad to us didn't mean that she wasn't trying to come up with a plan.

At first, running a store was a good venture for my dad. He seemed to like the role it gave him in our community. When we'd pull up to deliver a bag of groceries to the beautiful homes with careful landscaping, he seemed to swell when his regular customers would greet him by name. "Hi Gene! How's everything going?"

"Can't complain," he'd say as he passed over the brown paper bags filled with eggs, bread, and milk.

It was important to my dad to be important to others. And in this way, he was.

It turns out, however, that drinking until passing out every night makes it hard to run a successful business. Dad started showing up late to open in the morning and missing deliveries, which soured relationships with his customers as well as the suppliers who were trying to drop off the stock we needed. Empty shelves, inconsistent hours, then add in the bruises on his family members/employees and you can see why the business started to drop off. Sales declined steadily. Eventually they had to close the store.

Being so small, I can't say for sure that the stress of failure made things worse at home, but Dad's violence did seem to escalate at that point. And because of that, our situation was about to change.

My mother searched for a job she could do around town to help bring money in, and she started doing laundry for a gentleman in town who had six kids. His name was Abraham (not his real name).

Abraham and Mom started up a close personal relationship as she grew to know him and his kids better. Unbeknownst to my dad, Abraham offered my mom the love, support, and shelter she'd been missing. Finally, there was a safe harbor out there for her and her children.

One of my last memories of my father is of the night we tried to get away from him. The house was smoky again and it smelled of booze (as usual). My father had fallen asleep/passed out in front of the TV. With *Bonanza* blaring in the background, Mom waited until Dad had slept through at least one commercial break, then decided that this was our moment. It was time to make our escape.

Her eyes darted around the house, locating each of us in turn. "Now, let's go! It's time to leave," she whisper-shouted.

"Wait . . . what?" I said, having dozed off in Carol's room.

"Now! Get to the car!"

No "grab your coat." No "find your shoes." Do not collect your $200, just go!

Mom gathered us all up and we literally ran to the car. It only took me a second to go from almost asleep to running for my life.

Just as our fingers reached for the door handles on the battered station wagon, we heard a bellow from the house. Like an angry bear, roused from his nap, our father had awakened and, in three bounds, was right behind us running towards the car.

Loaded into the front and back seat, we all screamed, "Go, Mom! Go!" while her shaking hands fumbled to locate the right key and get it into the ignition. We all turned to check Dad's progress and noticed my window was down.

"Roll it up, Lori!" Keri screamed. If you've never had the pleasure of cranking up the window of a sixties-era sedan, let me tell you that it can be an arm workout, especially if the owner of the arm is five years old. Now, like my mom, I too was fumbling trying to get the window up while everyone yelled. Sitting right behind the driver's seat, I tried hard.

But I wasn't fast enough. Just as the car's wheels had started rolling backwards down the driveway, Dad's hand came through the opening and grabbed a fistful of my mom's long, dark hair. Rather than be pulled through the back window, she was forced to stop the car.

He beat her bad that night, just another night at the Price household. Listening to the cries and shouts, I felt so responsible for my mom getting beaten. If only I could have gotten that window up quicker! If I'd just been faster, we could've gotten away. I made a promise to myself and to my mother that night that I would try to protect her for the rest of my life. No matter what it took, I would be there for her.

The way I processed that incident with the window stuck with me for the rest of my life. My failure to protect my mom in that moment planted a seed within me that would continue to grow into an outsized sense of personal responsibility. Only now can I see how upside-down it is for a kindergartener to be responsible for the safety of an adult. At the time, it seemed like her protection would have to be up to me, come what may.

The night we almost made it out wasn't our last attempt at escape. Eventually, Mom succeeded in getting us four kids and herself to Abraham's house. Under his protection, Mom grew the confidence to sever ties with the man who had beaten her for more than a decade.

It took some time, but I have to give her credit. Mom did it. She left Dad, and he never bothered any of us ever again. Under Abraham's roof, I felt so protected. We were finally safe.

CHAPTER 3

We moved into the town of Elsberry and lived with Abraham and his six kids. Some might think that ten kids in one house would be overwhelming, but it wasn't. Not to me, anyway. I thought it was amazing! There was always someone to play with, someone to talk to; five girls and five boys was a sweet deal. Best of all, I felt safe there.

I can remember an early dinner with the whole group. There wasn't a ton of room in the dining area, but we squeezed in on benches. Mom made hot dogs every Friday, my favorite. At first, I remember that funds were tight and we just wrapped sandwich bread around our dogs. Then, as Mom and Abraham's income improved, we were able to afford real buns—a big deal to a kid. Finally, the day came that Mom added chili to the Friday offerings. Every Friday night without fail, those good chili dogs were sometimes the highlight of my week.

But that first big dinner, I was still getting used to this new kind of chaos. Being surrounded by eleven other people all talking and laughing was a first. My pigtails tied with thick yarn whipped me in the face as I looked left and right, trying to take it all in. The end of that day concluded not with alcohol and violence but with playing catch in the yard. I was in heaven.

As all of us kids became acquainted and got used to one another, I started to relax. I would pop out of bed in the morning, first one up, and hang out in the kitchen with a smile on my face just listening to people coming and going, taking turns in the bathroom, fixing themselves toast or cereal. It felt like we had pulled off a magic trick. I'd been in terrible danger, and now all of a sudden, I was surrounded by helpers. There were all these reasonable people who worked together to make a fulfilling life. Having lots of people around me made me feel safe and comfortable. I loved this new family.

My new family was active in sports. Mom and Abraham would go to the local games; they particularly liked Khoury softball and baseball, so everyone signed up to play for a league. At age five, I was still too young to play but I sure loved the Sun Drop sodas that were sold at the concession stand. That super-sweet yellow elixir made my head buzz. It was so good. I love it still today.

One particular May night, my family was watching my brother play baseball; I had wandered over to buy a soda and noticed the big kids were playing. Their eight and nine years to my five seemed so mature and cool. The baseball diamond, of course, had a concession stand, and they were building new bathrooms. Today, a construction site would be fenced off, but this being 1970, the rebar and concrete structure sat open to anyone who wanted to investigate . . . or climb! Next to the new bathrooms was a big pile of sand. It was almost like they had designed an obstacle course for us. Of course, the big kids were scaling the unfinished structure, then jumping off it into the sand pile, a leap of maybe seven feet.

So, as a junior member of this rag-tag assembly, I had a decision to make. *Do I try it? Do I make those eight- or nine-year-olds, my idols, think that I am an equal?* Yes! I am brave. It was time for me to get my Evel Knievel on and take the plunge.

I slowly climbed to the top, took a deep breath, and leaped! I jumped off! Into the pile of sand! Sweet success. On the way down, I had a second to relish my victory. I was Spiderman leaping around a city, a crime-fighting superhero. But when I landed and rolled to the ground, my right elbow thwacked against a hidden brick. There were probably three or four cubic yards of sand in that pile and just one brick. Of course, I hit it.

I was in instant pain and my tears welled. I didn't—couldn't—cry in front of my idols (you know, the eight- or nine-year-olds), so I ran back to my mother. By the time I got to her, I was sobbing hysterically the pain was so bad. My mom arranged for someone to take my brother home. We were off to the emergency room.

I remember hurting so much in the hospital I was crying and screaming, a five-year-old banshee. Carol came to the emergency room to see if I was OK. She didn't have to ask where I was, she just followed the sounds of my screams.

They took an x-ray of my elbow, and sure enough I had dislocated it. Then, the doctors had to set my arm, pulling the dislodged pieces into place, which caused excruciating pain through my body. Eventually they nestled my arm in a soft cast inside a sling. It was over. When you see little kids sporting a cast on their arm, they seem so cute, but I am here to tell you it's miserable for the kid.

For my final months of kindergarten, I had to try to sit very carefully at the table while writing my letters with my right hand

and cradling that left arm to my chest. The teachers were all very kind and everyone helped me. One of my neighbors was a boy named John who was also in kindergarten. He brought me candy and a six-pack of root beer as a gift. That's what friends are for.

For most of my life, I was cared for by my older sister, Carol. I called her my big sister, but to be honest, she was my primary caregiver as my mother was very busy trying to provide for us. Don't ask me how an 11-year-old dealt with raising a toddler, but she did.

She was always the person who took care of me. Once, when I was three or four, I had tagged along with Carol to a friend's house. They had Oreo cookies as a snack, which impressed my little-kid sensibilities to no end. Well, upon waking up in the night, and remembering those wonderful cookies, I left our house, went to that friend's, walked into their kitchen, and was found sitting in the dad's chair, eating their Oreo cookies at 2:00 a.m.

Another time, Carol and her friends were trying to pierce each other's ears using potatoes. When they got to Carol Jean's turn, I started screaming bloody murder. The girls pierced only one ear before they had to stop because I thought they were hurting my sister. Poor Carol, she was so patient with me. We left and she had to get her ears evened out another time.

By the time we moved to Abraham's house, Carol was 15 and I was five. Being the youngest kid in the entire household meant I was in kind of a hurry to show that I was no baby (thus the busted arm from the sandpile).

In first grade, I got to thinking about how all the other big kids in our household were so independent. Carol had an actual driver's license by then. But even ones who couldn't drive rode their bikes to baseball practice, to after-school jobs; they played with kids in other neighborhoods, forever leaving me—the baby—behind. But I was big too. I could do brave things.

I decided that I was way too big to have someone picking me up from the bus stop each day. The short walk home was well within my power, I thought. During one of our many talks, I told Carol I didn't need her to meet me anymore. I was a big girl now, I was six.

The next day when I got off at my stop, I remember my confidence lasted exactly two of the three giant bus stairs down to the ground. Standing on the sidewalk, amid the other kids jostling and joking, I suddenly felt very small. Scanning for Carol, I started to panic. Uh oh. She wasn't there. I became very scared and started crying uncontrollably. I threw my body on the ground and demanded that someone get my sister. She came running to the bus stop, asking me to stop crying, and gave me comfort.

"Lori, sweetie, don't you remember? You asked me not to come yesterday."

I sniffed, wiped my nose on my sleeve, and said, "I changed my mind."

That was the only time she did not pick me up from the bus stop. I felt safe when Carol was there for me.

My adopted family and I had a big old station wagon that we all piled into for road trips. I remember the long drives out west to see family. To save money, we'd eat sandwiches from a cooler and, as a treat, some grape soda. As the youngest, it was my job to squish in the back next to the cooler, but I didn't mind since it also meant I got to keep watch over the stash.

At least once a year, we visited Abraham's father, who lived in a small town in Colorado. He was glad to have the help on his large farm. My brothers would climb up on tractors and harvesters trying to get the crops in and mount up on horseback to manage the farm. All of this work was led by Abraham, of course. As a little squirt, my days on the farm were filled with chasing chickens (when no one would notice and yell at me) and climbing around inside the barn. We all enjoyed going to Colorado. It was quite beautiful with the great Rocky Mountains in the background and the dark night skies with so many stars.

One of our last trips to Colorado was a sad one. Abraham's father had died, and he and his siblings had to go there to make final arrangements and clear out the homestead. I don't remember who got the dining table or the family china, but the beloved family dog came back to Missouri with us. Josevus, Joe for short, was a smart and patient collie who tolerated all the pets and hugs we inflicted on him. We loved him. And I think he loved us too.

Suburbia was probably a big change for Joe, compared to the acres he'd had charge of in Colorado. But that dog was the most easygoing creature we ever owned. Around us kids, he was our protector, always close by. It was like he had swapped chicken duty for kid patrol and liked it just as well.

When I was six, Carol's life changed drastically. She had been dating a young man named Ronnie. At 17, she got pregnant, married Ronnie, and moved in with her new family. The early pregnancy wasn't considered a big deal in our family. We were all in love with her precious baby boy, Tony, who was so fun for me to visit and hold. And Ronnie and I became buds. He'd always get me raw chocolate-chip cookie dough to eat. (I still stand by the notion that anybody who says they don't love chocolate-chip cookie dough is lying.) I loved it and loved Ronnie for making that tradition. Carol's new family was so full of love and I was happy for her. I missed her at home, though. In her absence, I doubled my attempts to connect to my mom. As much as Carol Jean took care of me, there was always a connection to my mom. I loved her deeply. Still do.

On school breaks, we continued road-tripping to visit family. My mom's relatives lived in Phoenix and Los Angeles. It was twenty-two hours from Elsberry to Arizona. You might think we kids dreaded the time trapped in the car, but I liked road trips, they were fun. Mom would get us coloring books, crayons, and word search books. I also loved looking out the window and watching the terrain go from rolling hills in Missouri, to the flatlands of the prairie, to the majestic mountains of the great West.

We would stop for a few days in Phoenix where my Great-aunt Deena lived with her children. We loved playing with her kids for the short time we were there. A few times, they could join our caravan and trek along to Los Angeles.

Having grown up in a small town, Los Angeles, California seemed so exotic. I loved the tall buildings, seeing all the different kinds of people, and my mom's family, especially. For their privacy, I'm calling my aunt and uncle, Dave and Trudy. They also had three kids, and all of us kids were inseparable. It was like Camp Cousin, 24/7. We would go to the beach, and the feel of the cold water was exhilarating. Looking out, it was so vast, so intriguing, and so powerful yet so, so beautiful. It made me feel small but in a good way, in an "I'm one among many" way.

When we were tired of the beach, our parents would take us to downtown LA. Olvera Street was always top on our list. It's a historic district in the heart of Los Angeles that is built to resemble a Mexican village. The street is lined with shops and booths that are filled with brightly colored blankets and flowers. Best of all are the food stalls. The smell of taquitos and tacos alone was worth coming back for, time and time again.

Olvera Street stands out in my memory, but just as vivid is the food at Aunt Trudy and Uncle Dave's house. At least once a visit, they would crank up the grill for *carne asada*, marinated and grilled flank steak, served in warm tortillas with all the Mexican fixings. I think my mom loved revisiting her culture when we saw family, though when we'd get back to the Midwest, she would go right back to meat and potatoes, feed-the-farmer food. Even though she was dark complected, Mom didn't nurture her heritage beyond making a pan of enchiladas here and there; she'd have had to work at it if she'd wanted to. Family lore says my grandfather immigrated from Mexico and, raising his family in the United States, he refused to let anybody speak Spanish because he wanted his children to assimilate quickly. Living in LA, Mom's sister Trudy was able to learn more about Mexican culture and cooking, and I always looked forward to our visits to her home.

I have fond memories of seeing my extended family once a year. All of us kids were getting older. Each year, it was fun seeing which cousin grew the tallest, or who had pimples on their face, or who had the biggest boobs. Comparing, we would all laugh and tease about these developments.

I had no idea that we weren't the only ones who noticed we were changing.

CHAPTER 4

By the time I was 11, most of the 10 kids in our blended family had grown up and moved out. Those who still lived at home were older and busy with their own lives. The hustle and bustle of our first days all together was gone.

But that was OK; as a preteen, I figured I was quite mature and ready to handle my own problems. Although, my school performance didn't show that. I was a below-average student, getting mostly C's and D's. Looking back, I can see now that growing up in such a violent home had rattled me. The legacy of trauma meant my attention span was poor, and I felt anxious all the time, no matter what was going on. I was pretty messed up and just went through the motions when it came to schoolwork. A part of my brain was still on the lookout for trouble.

School was where I met my buddies, though. My friends Jeanette and Susan and I would go to movies or hang out at my house after school most days. There were two old cars in the garage where we'd climb behind the wheel and take turns pretending to drive. Being cool takes practice, we figured. Better start early.

Since every adult in my house was an avid smoker, cigarettes were easy to come by. Mom and Abraham both worked a lot; I didn't think they noticed the few smokes I swiped here and there.

My friends and I experimented with smoking wherever we thought no one would see, hiding out to smoke at the creek or in the bushes. Believe it or not, we even smoked on school property in the girls' bathroom.

Though I thought it wouldn't happen, the inevitable addiction did take hold. Soon enough, I wasn't smoking because I wanted to, but because I felt like crap if I didn't. Hooked as a preteen, I'd get headaches and felt so anxious if I couldn't scrounge up a Viceroy or a Salem by lunchtime. I loved them.

Picking up a smoking habit felt like the fulfillment of a family tradition. It almost seemed like I was expected to eventually start. Not that any adult ever introduced a child to smoking; they would often say we shouldn't try cigarettes. But every kid in the family eventually found their way to the habit. Part of that, I'm sure, was the era and the small town. In the seventies, you could smoke anywhere, restaurants, movie theaters, even the hospital. And in a small town, teens were short on other diversions; you were either an athlete, or you smoked . . . or you did both!

Where Elsberry kids had athletics or smoking behind the bleachers, the adults had Red's, the greasy spoon where my mom worked full time. She took orders and ran the grill, keeping folks supplied with burgers and tacos. She said she liked the work pretty well. Ruling over the counter, coffee pot in hand, Mom was an important person. People would come in both for a burger and to talk to her. Mom mostly covered the day shifts, except on Wednesday. That day Mom played in a bowling league during the day, then went to work for the evening shift.

Abraham usually worked days as well at the cement plant, so on Wednesdays, we were the only two at home. My sisters and brothers were all in activities or Abraham would give them money to go to the movies.

Abraham had this thing about wearing only a robe after his showers when he would get home, especially on Wednesdays. He would camp out in a chair in the living room, watching TV, and might innocently ask questions about my friends. If his interest in me seemed weird at the time, I shrugged it off. I didn't know to worry about it yet. Over time, I started to feel less comfortable with Abraham. It was like his fatherly attention had curdled somehow. What used to seem like friendly indifference was more intense attention.

One Wednesday, Abraham started asking about my friends again.

"Do Susan and Jeanette's parents know they smoke?"

Uh oh. "I . . . I don't know," I said.

"Lori, I know you're stealing cigarettes."

He just let that statement hang there while I struggled to swallow the lump in my throat. I had no idea what was going to take place, I just knew that I was in big trouble. If only I'd known then how much my life was going to change forever.

Abraham told me I needed to be spanked so he made me go to his bedroom. He told me to take my pants down so he could spank me. I sat there motionless for a long time until he shouted, "Do it!"

Terrified, I pulled my pants down, but tried to keep my underwear on.

"Those go too!"

Standing there, stiff as a board from the tips of my hair to the bottoms of my toes, my exposed butt hanging out for my stepfather to see, I felt humiliated and ashamed. Abraham spanked me, then kept his hands there on my buttocks after each strike, fondling me. I can't say how long this went on. Awhile. Long enough to completely shatter me physically and emotionally.

"You can leave now, but I'll be keeping an eye on you," he said.

I went straight to the bathroom, locked the door, and threw up.

Every Wednesday night, this would be my life. It started in the fall of the year I was 12 and didn't stop until I'd taken all the abuse I could bear. My anxiety and panic-filled days were all I knew anymore. Even on the rest of the days, I couldn't relax. He was in the house where I lived, and another Wednesday was coming again.

I didn't feel like I could tell my mom about this. I'd made a promise to her when I was five that I would protect her—with my life if needed. If she knew the truth about her husband, she would be crushed. My family would be torn apart, and it would be all my fault. I was carrying the weight of our family's happiness on my 12-year-old shoulders.

There were moments when my cortisol-filled body would feel like it just could not go on. I couldn't sleep, my grades got even worse, I felt absolutely rotten about myself for allowing this to happen to me. Some days I thought I might just do it; I might just tell Mom and end my nightmare. But it never felt like it was the right time. I didn't want Christmas to be ruined, or Easter to be in shambles. Every Sunday, all my brothers and sisters would come over to attend church together. After services, my mom would make a big country breakfast for everyone. Platters of bacon and eggs, and every sibling around the table . . . Mom was always so happy on those days. So, I kept my silence.

Instead, I tried to interrupt the Wednesday routine. I'd beg one of my brothers or sisters to stay home but they were all too busy.

"Sorry, Lori. I've got a game."

"Play practice…"

"Have to work!"

Or sometimes, they'd mysteriously find money for a spontaneous movie date. To this day I don't know if Abraham had anything to do with the number of activities they were all involved in. In the back of my mind, I know the answer.

One Wednesday evening, I asked my friend Sheila to spend the night with me so I wouldn't be alone with him. Since her parents wouldn't be home that night, her family said sure, that would be fun. I remember that evening specifically because when Abraham found out she was spending the night he whispered to me, "You're getting it bad next week for this."

Over time, my appearance worsened. Simple grooming was a chore. I didn't bathe regularly, and most of my friends went away. I heard they made a song about me called, "Cheesy Wanda." Psychologically, I was not well. I didn't care about my appearance or the odor that I'm sure lingered around my body. I actually wanted to be as ugly as possible so maybe the trauma and the abuse would stop. It didn't help the situation. My worst nightmare continued. The Wednesday meetings with Abraham continued through fall, winter, and on into the spring. I lived in a constant panic, constant fear. I had a sense of hopelessness during this period of my life.

Ever since I was a baby hiding in that closet, my whole life had been fearful. And like my mom before me, I had the sense that I just had to gut this out somehow. The model she had set for me was take, take, take until you can't take no more. Then, maybe, there would be a release. My mindset was that you have to wait until you hit your breaking point before you can find a way out.

Abraham started giving me gifts for my silence. A new stereo, more cigarettes: I always told him no, but it didn't seem to matter. One night, his approach shifted. Abraham told me that the next time, I would be lying on the bed while he was hitting and touching me. All while wearing just his robe. I was only 12, but I knew about sex. And I could tell that somehow Abraham was connecting these punishments to sex. The image of me lying on the bed with him touching me while wearing just a robe made something in me short-circuit. I knew I had to make it stop. I just had to figure out what I was going to do.

I knew for sure that I wasn't going to talk to my mom. I couldn't bear to see her face when I told my story. I mulled over in my mind all the trusted adults in my life. Not Mom . . . a teacher? No. Then, in a flash, I knew what to do.

My second-oldest sister, Keri, is the problem-solver of the family. If you needed anything, she either knew how to fix it or knew someone else who could help. She was always the planner, the organizer, the list-maker. I just knew she could figure out how to fix this mess. At that point, Keri and her husband had five kids all under the age of seven. They lived in Hannibal, but she usually visited once a week.

When her visit day came, I said to Keri, "Can I talk to you? In private?"

Once we were alone in my room, I sat motionless in a chair, kind of stuck for a moment. I didn't know where to start. If there was a before and an after in my life, this was the in-between spot. But then I couldn't stay stuck any longer. The tears in my eyes spilled over and the words came flooding out of my mouth.

I remember Keri's face shifted from curiosity to shock to sorrow as I shared the details of Abraham's Wednesday routine. She was horrified that I had been through so much physical and mental abuse.

"Oh, Lori. Are you OK?"

She must have said that half a dozen times. We were both crying. She asked my mom to come home from work so they could talk. Mom came home and disappeared into a spare bedroom with Keri. They must have been in there an hour. When they were done, Keri told me to pack some clothes; I was going to stay with her starting right now. I did not speak to my mother before I left but was already missing her.

Before we left, Keri called the Department of Social Services to report the abuse to the state of Missouri. I spoke with the social service worker when she came to Keri's house to interview me. Telling the story for the second time, it was easier. She was kind and reassuring. The woman taped the whole conversation, which lasted about an hour. She ended the conversation saying if he ever touched me again, the state of Missouri would prosecute him. That was the last time I spoke to anyone officially about my confrontations with Abraham. It wasn't until the writing of this book that I talked to Keri about that time (which is not good; families should talk about hard things). She told me that Social Services actually went to Abraham's work and threatened him with prosecution if the abuse continued.

I settled into living with my sister. Life at her house was peaceful. School was out for summer; I could just be still. My body started to relax again, though the anxiety that ramped up that year has never fully left me. The good thing was, I didn't have to be on high alert anymore. I started showering again and enjoyed getting to know my nieces and nephews.

Though Keri and Mom had talked about Abraham's behavior, I hadn't spoken to her about it until the day Mom came to visit me at my sister's house. Up to that point, there had been no communication from her about the situation. I was left feeling uncertain about my place in her affections, my place in the family. Yet, I still felt pulled to her. I just had to be by Mom's side. That childhood promise really stuck.

She said she was torn about having me come back to Elsberry or stay in Hannibal, but it was my decision to make. Mom promised I would never be alone with Abraham again. My grandmother (Mom's mom) was moving in to guarantee my safety.

I was very emotional. As much as I loved my sister, I needed my mother. And again, I was being put in a position of having to make adult decisions as a child. I couldn't say it out loud. I scribbled seven words on a napkin, "I need to be with my mom."

I did move back into the house, and sure enough my grand-mother was there to make sure I was safe. I was never truly alone with Abraham, ever again. So, in that way, Mom did fix the prob-lem. The abuse stopped. But that wasn't all that was broken, and looking back now, I can see she failed me in some ways.

In that conversation at Keri's, Mom said, "This is a family situ-ation. If we can't fix it, we won't be a family." I think we shouldn't have been a family. But I can also see that she didn't really mean to leave Abraham. She kept this secret hidden, even, I think, from my grandma who was there to protect me.

It only recently dawned on me that this was the only time that my mother and I talked about the situation, and she never said it wasn't my fault. She should have fought harder to help me feel whole and valued. She was my mother, and I was her child, her youngest. She should have done more. It's so disheartening to think about it, even now. I can see that her priority was to always stick by her man. She didn't feel able to put her children first. And she didn't.

CHAPTER 5

The first days of living back with my mom and Abraham were tense. I had this feeling that the peace Mom had brokered would fall apart at any second. It was such a tense situation in the house. There was an odd silence that stemmed from an unspoken rule that no one could talk about the abuse. I'm not sure if my mom was trying to pretend that it hadn't happened, or if she just wanted to keep moving forward and leave it behind.

At any rate, my grandma was there in the kitchen all the time now. She usually camped out at the table and crocheted endlessly. Seeing her there reminded me of better times, younger days, when she had made crocheted shawls for all of us girls, each one a different color. Best of all, she provided matching purses, all of which held four or five dollars in quarters. We thought we were rich at the time. With that money, we'd visit the arcade and play Pac-Man or stop by the candy house a couple of streets over. It might sound odd now, but in our small town, there weren't a lot of stores, so someone had set up a table on their porch to sell penny candy to the neighborhood kids. I'm sure we overpaid by quite a bit, but we didn't mind passing over a quarter for our favorites like Sixlets or Bit-O-Honey.

Though Abraham was still there, he knew why Grandma had moved in. He knew what he'd done was wrong and he kept his distance, though I could tell he was mad about it. From time to time, he'd snap at me or just glower, but Mom's solution did work. The abuse stopped. Eventually I began feeling better and taking better care of myself. Funny how a shower, deodorant, and not being assaulted can make a world of difference in a middle-schooler's life. I didn't really reconnect with my old friends but did make new ones. I befriended the class smart kids, Terry and Penny. My new friends were always very nice to be around and supportive of me. They had no idea the horrific tragedy I had endured at home. I hated talking about it, so I didn't.

With Terry and Penny's encouragement and example, I got more focused in school and started earning better grades. For the first time, I could really put my energy toward school. When I was finally able to fully pay attention, I realized I had missed some fundamentals. The rest of my class had learned how to do things like multiply fractions and identify cell parts without me, so I was way behind and had to hustle hard to get back to grade level. Within a few months I was on the B honor roll. I started feeling proud of myself and so did my mom. I don't know that my family situation can be called "normal" by most people, but it was my first taste of fear-free living and I loved it.

I started playing flute in the band and joined the volleyball team. At five foot nothing, I found that my ability to stay steady in tight spaces made me an excellent setter. I can remember loving being a part of the team and feeling proud that I was able to contribute to successful volleys: bump, set, spike! I was right there in the middle of the action. That happiness didn't even dim when I realized I could cross under the net by barely ducking my head.

That's not to say that my anxiety didn't crop up. The normal jitters that most people get before tests or a big game were building toward full-fledged panic attacks. My body was now wired to go from chilling to freaking out in mere seconds. I chewed my nails constantly, was a bit food obsessed, and smoked as often as I could. Smoking was the one thing that carved out a bit of space in my head. That first drag never failed to calm me; it was like, OK breathe, here's a bit of peace.

Having now lived past the age of 50 in a body that was programmed for fight/flight/freeze from the very beginning, I have learned that survivors of trauma will never quite feel at peace. Even when things really are OK, you can't quite believe it. Always, in every situation, I'm thinking of the worst-case scenario. *If I drive through this snowstorm, will I go off the road, land in a ditch, and die of exposure?* As an adult, I can now see such catastrophizing for the symptom that it is. As a teen, the thoughts seemed like real possibilities. *If I walk to the bus stop, is some crazed man going to kidnap me? When I get off the bus, will I slip and get run over by the bus?* Somewhere as a kid, I started living my normal life alongside every worst-case scenario playing out in my head. Unfortunately, though I no longer smoke or chew my nails, I still live in this head space most of the time.

While some of my thoughts are clearly unrealistic, I wasn't wrong to keep a watchful eye on Abraham. Years after becoming an adult, I learned that he had entered one of my sisters' rooms naked. She screamed, he left, and Mom explained it away as "confusion." Carol once explained that the reason she never moved back home permanently, even after she separated from her husband, was "not wanting to play his games," meaning that she'd had conflict with Abraham too. He did try to get handsy with me one last time when I was 13. Instead of freezing like I had before, I followed the instructions the social workers had given me. I straightened up to my full five feet in height, took a deep breath, and shouted, "NO!" Abraham took his hands off me and was never physically inappropriate again.

Believe it or not, I grew to feel safe enough at home that I let Abraham help me with my driver's education. The very first time I sat behind the wheel to actually drive a car, the two of us were in the driveway at our house.

"OK, Lori," Abraham said in a patient, fatherly voice. "Put it in reverse, give it a little bit of gas, and let's get out of the driveway."

So, I tried, but obviously not enough because the tires didn't even roll an inch.

"No, Lori, the gas," he said.

This time, we moved maybe two or three inches. This scenario happened probably four different times. Finally, Abraham lost his patience.

"Goddammit, Lori! Give the car some gas and get the car out of the driveway!" he yelled.

I punched it; we went flying backwards out of the driveway . . . right into the car that was parked across the street. *Oh shit.* I pulled the car back into the driveway, my maiden voyage having consisted of forty feet forwards and backwards with no turns. As Abraham was storming out of the car, he noticed Carol and Keri watching from the lawn, laughing their asses off.

"If you guys think it's so damn funny, you can pay for it yourselves," he said, and he slammed the door.

Despite that disastrous beginning, I eventually figured out how to drive safely. Since Elsberry was (and still is) a small town, population 2,000, my folks didn't really worry about me. They knew I couldn't get into much trouble, and if I did someone was bound to tell them about it. Even with the single stoplight and my mom behind the counter at Red's watching me cruise up and down the one main drag, driving felt like sweet, sweet freedom. I drove my chariot, a hunter-green Chrysler Cordoba, all over town listening to Lionel Richie on the radio, cigarette in hand.

Sixteen meant freedom: a driver's license, fun with friends, and—at least in our family—the ability to smoke openly. It was another thing no one talked about, you just kind of knew that at 16, you could smoke in front of our parents without getting in trouble.

As I said, baseball was a big deal at our house. Not only did most of my siblings play on local Khoury teams, but we all grew up Cardinals fans. I loved going to see games at Busch Stadium in downtown St. Louis. My mom would survey the family to see who wanted to go to games so she could order seats together. We'd sit in the loge-level seats, holding our dogs (with mustard) and Cokes, teasing each other, and waiting for our favorite players to bat. Busch Stadium held heat like an oven, so I remember it being really hot, but I enjoyed being there every time. It was one of those rare moments when I could relax and find some peace. There's something almost holy about the communal feel of a crowd at a game, everyone's attention focused on the same thing. "Go crazy, folks, go crazy!" the announcer would cue the crowds, and we would all yell as loud as we could. Cheering together, you can let the rest of the world slip away for a while.

Any serious St. Louis fan can tell you exactly where they were when the Cardinals beat the Milwaukee Brewers in the 1982 World Series. When the Brewers came to Busch Stadium, it was beers against beers. On that fateful night, I was sitting cross-legged in my usual spot on the living room floor with my back against the wall. I would watch the game intensely, while unconsciously gnawing off a cuticle or two. I cheered until I cried, the night they won that pennant. Of course, the Cardinals have won more championships since then, but the 1982 title was a special one, especially for me. It felt emblematic of that entire era of my life. I felt so free because I finally felt safe. I was free from Gene, free from Abraham, and on track to be successful in my life. While Kool & the Gang's "Celebration" played and everyone hooted and hollered, I felt like all was right with the world.

That World Series win happened in the fall of my senior year of high school, which was a fitting start for me. I had continued to struggle off and on with my grades, especially in my sophomore year. In my senior year, I had a few credits to wrap up in the morning, then in the afternoons, I would attend the CNA (certified nursing assistant) program in the vo-tech building. I found it fun to learn about anatomy and physiology and a little worrisome to learn about safety protocols. All the different ways you could inadvertently hurt someone were intimidating, but I was glad to have that certification under my belt before I even graduated. It felt like security.

Thinking back, there are a couple of factors that led me to the nursing profession. I do like helping people, I've come to find more and more meaning in my work as I've spent time in my field. But, in some ways, I ended up in healthcare because of the way our school's social classes sorted themselves. Remember, it was the early eighties. As a girl, you had two choices: you were either a secretary or a nurse. I knew I was a hard worker; I knew that I wanted to help people, so I became a nurse. Simple as that.

So, when the job fair rolled around in April, I did as my CNA instructors urged and visited the nursing booth. The Pike and Lincoln County area technical school was looking for a few good women to sign up for their licensed practical nursing program. Having already started a nursing assistant's course of study, I knew a bit about what I might be in for. Plus, there was the money to consider. I signed up for the fall schedule.

May 1983 was a very special time for me; I graduated from Elsberry High School! There were times in my freshman and sophomore years that I wasn't sure I was going to make it to that point. I felt like accomplishing this goal might have had something to do with the grace of God. The right people came into my life at the right moment. With their support, I did it!!

After graduation, I got to travel back to sunny California to visit my cousins and Aunt Trudy. Seeing them was as good as ever. This time, in addition to the food and the beach, I was surprised with a birthday and graduating gift to remember. I got to go see the St. Louis Cardinals play the Los Angeles Dodgers at Dodger Stadium. Sitting in the stands, singing, "Take Me Out to the Ballgame," I remember thinking my life was finally just how I wanted it to be.

CHAPTER 6

September 1983 found me sitting in a classroom, pen and paper in hand, jittery despite the cigarette I'd had on the way over. Being one of the younger students in class, my nerves were jangling all over the place. I can remember watching my instructor, crisp in her nurse's uniform, shuffling papers behind a podium, waiting for class to begin. I will never forget the first thing she said. "If you're going to become an LPN, you need to know these two rules." I sat up straighter, pen in hand, awaiting her wisdom.

"Rule number one . . . people are going to die . . . rule number two . . . you can't change rule number one."

I was stunned. *What in the heck have I gotten myself into?* I can remember looking up at the EXIT sign and considering leaving. I spent the rest of that class feeling a little rattled. It took a few days, but after the initial shock from her comments wore off, I settled into everyday school life. Having come straight to nursing school from my high school CNA program did make me young compared to the other LPN candidates, but it wasn't a disadvantage. I just went from one type of school to another, staying in study mode the whole time.

At the end of the school day, with anatomy terms and blood pressure statistics still swimming through my head, I would head over to Red's to work the evening shift. When things were slow, I'd sit on a stool at the counter and read a medical textbook until the next rush.

By this point, Abraham and Mom had bought out the previous owner of the diner. They hired a manager to run operations and a mix of local kids and me and my siblings to work the counter and the kitchen. I was too short to work the grill; my mom said you had to be a certain height to do that safely. So, I was always up front taking orders, running the register, and filling shake and ice cream orders.

One time, I was training a new girl from high school. She'd clearly spent some time getting ready for work that day. Her long, permed hair was curled, teased, and sprayed up high in that mid-eighties cotton-candy style. I was making a dip cone—soft-serve ice cream dipped in chocolate sauce that would harden. I remember pulling the cone out of the chocolate, turning around quickly to keep the drips off the floor, and connecting ice cream to hair all in one motion. She gasped as we both realized that I'd just crammed ice cream all through her hair. She was horrified, but I found it kind of funny. "You don't have to spend an hour on your hair to work at Red's," I told her later. "Stuff like that happens sometimes."

We all had chores to complete before we could leave each evening at close. Sweep and mop, refill the ketchup bottles . . . the one I hated the most was moving the ice cream machines to sweep and mop underneath. They were so heavy. Before everyone left, Mom or Abraham would come in to collect the cash register receipts and check our work. One night it was Abraham's turn to close. I knew

I was supposed to check with the manager about schedules, but Abraham was standing right there, so I asked him, "Is it OK if I leave? I'm done and need to get home and study."

"Ask the manager if you can leave," he snapped back in a snide voice.

The words on the page alone don't convey how mean he was being to me. That's how it always was those days between us. Our interactions usually consisted of me trying to placate or avoid him, Abraham glowering at me, no matter what I did until he saw a chance to vent his anger at me. He was so hateful at times it was hard to take, but I thought to myself, at least he wasn't physically touching me.

I can remember one day I was standing up in the customer area, cleaning one of the front windows when my mom came in the back door. Her rubber-soled shoes squeaked a little on the linoleum as she said, "Lori, I need to tell you something."

I put the rag down and looked at her. "I'm sorry to have to tell you this. I just heard that your dad died."

Gene, the man who had beaten Mom and terrorized me and my siblings for years, was dead. I'd only seen him a couple of times after we escaped from his house. Past age four, he'd really had no bearing on my life. It's funny, though. My sisters said if Gene had known what Abraham had done to me, he would have killed him.

Standing there in front of the No Shirt, No Shoes, No Service sign, my only thought was, *huh*. I wasn't sure how to feel about the death of my biological father. He had been living in Desert Hot Springs, California. Apparently, after a few too many drinks at the bar (again), he died in his car in his driveway, where he started decomposing in the heat. Due to the high temperatures in the valley there, and the fact that his body wasn't discovered for a few days, Gene was unrecognizable. Maggots had swarmed his body, leaving the coroner only the tattoo of my mother's name for positive identification. "Carol," it said. The car had to be totaled. Gene's body was cremated, and his ashes were spread over the Mojave Desert.

Gene had been living with his son, Richard, who has special needs. Richard is about ten years younger than me, so he was maybe 9 when this happened. We figured out after the fact that poor Richard probably saw his dad rotting there in the driveway and didn't know what to do. I can't imagine how scary that must have been for him. My older brother Ted took Richard in and raised him after that.

I remember wondering if I should be mourning this man, my biological father. I didn't feel sad that he was gone, just relieved. That was one person my mother and I never had to worry about for the rest of our lives. That bogeyman was gone. Thank God.

You'd think that with his death and Abraham leaving me alone, my days would be less stressful. And they were. My 18-year-old life was much more peaceful than the life I lived at age 4 or 12. However, starting out like I did leaves a mark. Even though things were relatively quiet, I still had periods of great anxiety. I almost wonder if the quiet was the reason for the heightened anxiety. Maybe my body only knew how to operate in panic mode. Now that I had found some peace, maybe my nervous system was trying to recreate the environment it had grown used to. I'd be driving to school and a panic attack would just wash over me. My heart would pound, my hands would shake, and it just felt like I couldn't breathe. I'd have to pull the car over until I could catch my breath again. Panic attacks and fear just washed over me at times. At this point I was able to successfully deal with them by waiting them out. But over time, all the feelings I had just stuffed down kept forcing their way to the surface. I couldn't control when they'd come.

Back in the eighties, seeing a psychiatrist was completely taboo. It crossed my mind that if I tried to seek help, I wouldn't be allowed to babysit my nephews any longer; it might even affect my ability to work in healthcare.

A panic attack feels like your body thinks you're dying. You could be lying in bed, just getting ready to go to sleep and instead of relaxing, your muscles start tensing up. Your heart rate speeds, as does your breathing. The killer thing about it is that your mind knows you are safe, yet it can't control the symptoms your body is kicking up. All those years of avoiding feelings don't just vanish.

By the time the panic attacks were so bad that I could barely function, I had finished my school semester and was just looking forward to a peaceful summer. Instead, I felt like every day I was walking through mud. I was barely making it for all the anxiety I kept dealing with. At school, work, and home, I had to go splash cold water on my face several times a day to hold it together.

Still, I didn't tell anyone about the building anxiety I was experiencing. I still lived with Mom and Abraham. Basically, all my brothers and sisters had moved out by then. It was just me and my two nephews, Tony and Ryan, left in the house. Many of my siblings would meet us at church every Sunday. We attended the Presbyterian church, and I can remember wishing it would go faster. I was hungry! Church with family seemed to fill my mom's soul up, but I suspect it was the breakfast afterward that she enjoyed more. Sunday breakfast was still a tradition that she reveled in. She usually made pancakes or eggs. Mom preferred simple feed-the-farmer type dishes that drew the crowd, week after week.

Looking around the table at all those fair-skinned Midwesterners, Mom and I kind of stuck out with our black hair and caramel-colored faces. They liked to give me a hard time about not looking anything like Carol, Keri, or Ted. "Ha! Lori, you must be the mailman's kid!"

Mom would just laugh and shake her head. She'd roll her eyes and say, "Who wants more bacon?"

But we did look different than everyone else in the family. One time, the KKK was coming through town to do some sort of event. Back then, they did parades and rallies right out in the open. Our family friends told Mom and Abraham that Mom and I should stay at home inside the house that day.

I had to work hard to make good grades in nursing school. It was extremely difficult, and I was taking it very seriously. As I was making my way through, I ran into an old friend of mine, Missy, from my high school days. Her boyfriend was coming for a visit from his home in Omaha. She said he was bringing a friend and asked if I'd like to join them on a double date. I hadn't had much experience dating but I said sure, "Why not?"

Ken showed up to pick me up seeming nervous but very nice. He had a lanky, slender build and wore his facial hair in a mustache and beard. "Hello, you must be Lori," he said, then swallowed hard.

The four of us went for dinner and a movie and we had a great time. While Ken was in town, the two of us went out several more times. We were very compatible and enjoyed many of the same things, like pop music and quiet nights. He was a big car fan; I remember kind of faking enthusiasm about it for his benefit. He was my first boyfriend, and I was so excited. When Ken left to go back home to Omaha, we said we'd write and visit as much as we could, and we did just that. The letters and care packages we sent back and forth flooded our mailboxes. He'd send me mixtapes with songs he thought I might like. I remember, "Money for Nothing" by Dire Straits on one of them. Since I was still in nursing school, his letters were a good diversion. I would save a new letter to open until I was done with my homework like you save dessert for last. I'd look up from my desktop studies and there sat the white envelope with Ken's cramped blue writing, waiting for me.

After eighteen months of classes, I graduated from nursing school in December of 1984. I wore a blue-and-white striped uniform with my nursing cap to the graduation ceremony. Ken couldn't make it, but my mom was there. I couldn't believe it was over. I was so relieved and proud of myself. All I had to do now was pass the state board exam; then I would be a licensed practical nurse with the state of Missouri.

While I was studying to take the state board test, Ken and I had been talking about the idea of me moving to Omaha. I didn't like the idea of leaving my mother, but I'd also grown very fond of and very close to Ken. So, I put that deep worry about protecting my mom to the side and made the leap. I was going to do it! Omaha or bust.

When I took my state board exams, I also inquired about a Nebraska nursing license, which they told me was a simple matter of paperwork. Great! Now all I had to do was wait on my test results. I walked to the mailbox every day hoping for some word about my test. Every day I would open the mailbox only to be let down that the letter wasn't there. My fear and anxiety about passing built. What if I failed? I wouldn't be able to get a job, and without a job, I couldn't move to Omaha to be closer to Ken. Everything depended on passing that test, and why couldn't they just send the darn results?!

One day, the mailbox contained more than coupons and bills. I reached in and . . . there it was: that familiar mix of fear, anxiety, and horror. It tasted like metal and shallow breathing. I had learned to deep breathe through these episodes. While I stared at the letterhead printed with State of Missouri Nursing Licensure, these thoughts raced through my head: *Did I just waste the last eighteen months of my life? What if I mess up and cause someone to fall and get hurt?* I breathed in through the nose, out through the mouth . . . Once my heart rate felt less like a rattly old engine and more like a human's, I was able to open the letter . . . I PASSED!!!

CHAPTER 7

The feelings of exhilaration lasted maybe one minute. I was definitely proud of myself after all the work I'd put in. But the words of that first-day instructor still haunted me. *Rule number one: people are going to die.*

The realization that I was going to be responsible for other people's lives made me doubt myself again. I was petrified that I might do the wrong thing. So, I did what any girl in my position would do . . . I signed up for more shifts at Red's, of course. I was so scared of hurting somebody; I couldn't work as a nurse.

This decision lasted approximately four months. As I swept and mopped floors, tallied up lunch tickets, and mixed shakes, I began to think about the education I was wasting. I realized that God had given me the gift of patience and a love for people. My instructors had all given me positive comments and grades. I knew I could do the work of a licensed practical nurse. I applied at a local nursing home in Troy, Missouri. I was still scared but was determined to make a difference in someone's life.

When I started working, I fumbled at first, as all beginning nurses do. I was green and patients didn't look like the textbook scenarios that I had been given. I'd be checking on a patient who'd spiked a fever when the doctor would walk in and expect a report. "What is she on?" he would ask, referring to a patient's medications.

"Uhhh, I don't know." I felt dumb when that would happen. I did know there was an antibiotic onboard but didn't have the whole list of usual pharmacological options in my head then like I do now. These days when I'm training brand-new nurses, I always tell them to have all their information in line before speaking to the doctors. Get their vital signs and diagnoses together and meds straight. Basically, get your head organized so you can sound like you know what you're talking about.

As the weeks went on, I grew more confident. I started making strong connections with patients that helped me feel like I really was helping them. They seemed happy to see me and said they appreciated the way I could help them feel safe and not so scared.

Though my confidence grew, I was still terrified of making a mistake that would kill somebody. Thank God that never happened.

Ken and I were still crazy about one another. We went back and forth visiting each other between Elsberry and Omaha. He was just learning to be a truck driver, so the miles were good practice for Ken, but in the long run I wanted to be closer to my new love.

I applied for a Nebraska state nursing license and got it. It was hard telling my mother I was leaving. I had sworn to myself that I was here to protect her and here I was, moving away. But she was in a good place with Abraham, Gene was dead, and her kids were all adults now. Deep inside I knew Mom was OK.

I found that I kind of liked Omaha. I lived a block away from Dodge Street right next to the Mutual of Omaha headquarters. I had a quaint little apartment and a job at a nursing home. Selecting the best cupboard for my hand-me-down plates and getting ready each day in my very own apartment, I felt very grown up.

Ken and I would see each other when we could. He still lived with his parents, which made sense since he was now an over-the-road truck driver. Those long-haul trips meant that there were times I was alone but that was OK. During those nights alone in the apartment, I learned that I kind of liked solitude. I'd never had a place all to myself. It was nice to be in charge of the radio and TV, nice to control what kinds of food were in the fridge; it suited me.

Ken had a friend, Nick, who became my friend too and the three of us hung out a lot together. Nick was in the car racing business. He would tear up the dirt track on Sunday nights in the local stock car races. The stands were packed for these events; it seemed like lots of folks really looked forward to watching Nick and his colleagues compete. I definitely did; it was a little scary, though. I remember one time Nick's car stalled on the track and he got out to see what the problem was—right on the track! Ken and I clutched each other's hands that night, fearful Nick would be hurt. He wasn't. The man had a guardian angel.

One day that summer, we three drove Nick's hot Mustang back to Missouri to catch a Cardinals game. Ken was trying to show an interest in the things I loved, so when he showed up that morning wearing all red, I swallowed a laugh. Red shirt. Red pants. Even a red hat. It was about that point that I started to think of Ken as a bit of a dork. I felt annoyed that I would have to take this tomato of a guy to my favorite place in the world. My people, my tribe of Cardinals fans were all going see him and roll their eyes. *Oh boy, it's going to be a long day,* I thought. We still got dogs and beers and had fun, but cracks were forming in our relationship.

Stuck in Omaha, I spent my first and last Christmas away from my mother in 1985. That was a hard day. I volunteered to work that day to let people who could, stay home with their families. I did call home after my shift, but I told my mother leading up to Christmas that I would only speak to her on the phone if we didn't actually say the word Christmas.

"So . . . thanks for the box," I said.

"Oh! You're welcome. Do the boots fit?"

"Yeah." I was so sad. It was hard for both of us. Family get-togethers were such a big deal in my family. I hated that I was missing all my siblings and their families, and especially my mom.

Ken's job, of course, took him out of town a lot. I expected that but didn't realize until I'd already moved to Omaha that his mother still kept a tight leash on her 25-year-old boy. This meant that even though he'd been gone and wanted to come see me, many nights he would have to stay home with her instead. I didn't realize at first that it was his mom who *wouldn't let him go out.* I had started to wonder if he was losing interest. Then, visiting their home for dinner (her homemade spaghetti sauce was excellent), I'd see how she would order Ken around.

Just as he was trying to sit down with me, from the kitchen would come an order. "Ken, go fetch that paper for me." Up he'd run and fetch. The second he returned she'd issue another command. "Ken, take the trash out." It was like that all night long. I'd had no idea his mother was this controlling. It began to be a problem for us. Ken's mother and I were competing for his time and attention. Based on Ken's behavior, I knew I was going to lose this battle.

It was weird, though. In the beginning, it was Ken's mom who paid for my plane ticket to Omaha to come surprise him. She just told him to come with her to the airport to "pick up a friend," and there I was smiling at baggage claim. He was delighted. I didn't know what had happened to shift things so drastically.

Eventually I got into a shouting match with my boyfriend's mother about being able to spend time with him. The relationship was over that night. I was done trying to get a grown man to cut himself free from the apron strings. Fifteen months into living in Omaha, I was on my own.

Though I no longer had a boyfriend, I still had a lease, which meant I couldn't just up and move without losing my deposit. I was in Omaha and alone for my twenty-first birthday that May. Where does a St. Louis girl go to toast her twenty-first birthday? Bob Gibson's sports bar, of course—the place named after one of my favorite Cardinals Hall-of-Famers. I sat at the bar and ordered a beer, looking around at the wood-paneled walls. My eyes focused on the Omaha skyline, reflected in the barback mirror. Raising a glass to myself, I said, "Go crazy, folks, go crazy," and settled in to have a few.

Finally, I moved back home. I got an apartment in Elsberry and a nursing job in St. Charles, about forty miles away. It was a commute that many people in town made and no one seemed to mind. I did feel better being back home and liked the place I'd rented pretty well, but somehow, I couldn't shake my building anxiety. I'd been smoking since I was 14 years old and at this point was a regular chimney. And then there were the dreams.

Especially after my breakup with Ken, I can remember a recurring dream I had where I was driving a car, going up a hill. I can't see over the top and don't realize that there is water on the other side until I've crested the hill, but by then I'm going too fast to stop. My car plummets down the road and right into the water, where my car sinks and I drown. Every time I have that one, I wake up in a sweat, shaking. I think it's about the feeling of impending doom that I carried with me, always. I still feel that way today, like I'm always expecting the worst to happen. I need to get over that, though thankfully, I haven't had that dream in a long time.

To fill my time and ease the anxiety, I started frequenting an Elsberry bar named The Red Door. They had live music on the weekends, and I enjoyed going, even by myself. Looking back, maybe I enjoyed going too much; I became enough of a regular that the bartender knew my drink order.

"Hey, Lori! Tom Collins?" he'd ask.

"Mmmm . . . make it a White Russian tonight," I'd say, feeling worldly and sophisticated at age 21.

I learned about the bar scene in those months. Dating people who hang out at bars turns out not to be an ideal way to find long-term romance. It should be obvious, but that's the beauty of being young. You think the rules don't apply to you. I dated a few men from the bar, but nothing ever materialized with anyone. There was one man who I absolutely adored. His name was Larry. He lived in St. Louis but had a weekend cabin on the river. I think I irritated him more than anything because he never took the hints I dropped about "being so lonely," or "wishing something fun would happen." I'm so socially awkward, I tend to do the wrong thing.

Poor, naïve 21-year-old Lori. I really wasn't thinking clearly. Instead of just going up to him and saying, "Hi, Larry. I like you. Let's go out for dinner," I dated his friends and acquaintances. Why?! I was attempting to make him jealous. You'll be shocked to learn that nothing ever happened between Larry and me. I think that was an opportunity lost.

One perk about being back in Elsberry was getting to see my nieces and nephews grow up, though it was bittersweet for me. My brothers and sisters were all having children of their own, and I loved being Aunt Lori. One of my stepbrothers had married; he and his wife had two girls and a boy and made the cutest family. I used to babysit for them a lot. I enjoyed it and needed the extra cash, but I really wanted to have my own children, my own family to love.

It got so bad sometimes; I would just be consumed with envy, especially at the once-a-month get-togethers. Most of the ten siblings would come and bring their spouses and children. There would be music and barbecue, kids swinging on swings and throwing balls to each other. I felt left out. Again. Standing on the outside of things, I was so jealous and so sad. I wanted someone to love so bad—a daughter or a son of my own.

These feelings of sadness, panic, and fear were so close to the surface all the time. They were about much more than sibling rivalry and worry about the way my life was turning out. But I didn't know that at the time. At the time, it seemed like I was the only one in my family who was lonely. Everyone else was married and having kids, and here I was still working and living alone. My twenties were passing me by and no one, it seemed, was interested in me. *Would anyone ever want me,* I wondered. It was deeply disappointing. Yet, I didn't have any power over who found me attractive or wanted to date me. I felt stuck.

When I wasn't dreaming about drowning, I dreamt that I was standing in the front yard of my parents' home in Elsberry. I would be taking very careful steps across the yard, making sure to place my feet exactly on the steppingstones so I didn't slip off. Right as I looked at my feet, I'd realize that the ground—except for the stones—was completely covered in snakes. Petrified of moving, I would stand stock still. Marooned on my tiny island.

Eventually the panic attacks seeped from my dream world into my waking world. I was back to splashing my face at work to calm down, but it wasn't cutting it. I went around with dread in my gut all day long. I was an emotional wreck. After several days in a row with little sleep, my body exhausted by the tension and adrenaline, I muttered aloud the words that had been running through my head: "I would be better off dead." When I heard that phrase come out of my mouth, I scared myself. I knew I had to get help.

I went to the hospital emergency room. By the time I walked in the door, I was sobbing so hard I was physically sick. I was put in the psychiatric unit of St. Peter's hospital on a direct admit, where I stayed for three or four weeks. It was a communal wing for psychiatric patients with group therapy, a TV room, and dining room. At first, I stayed in my room and did not want to talk to anyone. Maybe my mom but that was it. I definitely didn't want to talk to the other patients. My fear of tragedy, panic attacks, and anxiety was front and center.

I kept trying to close my door completely, but for safety reasons, that wasn't allowed. The nurses were all top-notch; they made it their mission to make all of us feel as comfortable as possible. After a few days, I started leaving my door all the way open and heard the other patients talking and laughing in the TV room. Once I could breathe again, I slowly found myself gravitating towards them. I joined the *General Hospital* viewing group with all their joking about the improbability of the plot lines. I remember realizing that I was smiling and laughing with my newfound friends and didn't know how long it had been since I'd done that.

Every day I was visited by the medical doctor, the psychiatrist, and went to group therapy with my new friends. I felt uncomfortable talking about myself and my past. Some of the things I expressed were strictly on the do-not-talk-about list! Somehow, I was able to share the things I had experienced because of Gene and Abraham, and I was surprised that it seemed to ease the burden a little.

The doctors ended up giving me a diagnosis of post-traumatic stress disorder and depression. I started taking medication immediately. After almost a month, I felt my self-confidence return. I felt balanced again. I still had anxiety and panic in my life, but I learned how to deep breathe and relax.

I started to feel like an old pro at panic attacks. When they would happen, I'd think about the techniques the psychiatrist taught me. *Just calm down, Lori,* I'd tell myself. *Put yourself in a neutral place and think about things that are positive in your life.* Those techniques coupled with my medication made all the difference in the world. I was feeling better.

An important point that I learned from my stay in the hospital is that depression and anxiety will always be with me. My approach before the stay—wishing they would go away—isn't a good wellness strategy. It's not weakness to ask for help. Rolling into the emergency room that day with "just feelings" as my symptoms was really scary. I now think of that as one of the bravest things I've ever done. The help I got from all the doctors and nurses who cared for me saved my life.

I started accepting visitors during my hospital stay. I was very fearful that my oldest brother and his wife would not let me see their children because of my breakdown and my diagnosis. To my surprise, they were accepting of me and supportive. I was so relieved and happy to know that they saw me for who I was and still loved me. I was still keeping the secret about Abraham. I never did have a conversation with any of my brothers or sisters except Keri and Carol regarding the abuse I had suffered. Though I was able to share that with my group therapy friends, I kept that part of the family story on the do-not-talk list with most everyone at home. The family culture of keeping hardships to yourself ran deep, and I didn't want Abraham's kids to have to carry the burden of what he'd done to me.

After I was discharged from the hospital, I had every intention of keeping in contact with my newfound friends but as it was, we never made contact again. I think that the bubble of safety and security we formed evaporated once we were back in our real lives, on our own again.

CHAPTER 8

I spent the rest of my twenties perfecting my craft. I was trying to be the best nurse and person I could be. Nursing has become my vocation both because I really feel useful to others, and because it gives me a strong sense of pride. I think the best nurse is one who allows herself or himself to learn every day and attempt to put their best foot forward every day. That's how I try to approach each and every shift. I think of myself as a servant to others.

There's a saying we often talk about at work that goes: "And the patient said, 'Send in a miracle. Help me, God.' And in walks a nurse." I'm here to help. I can't save the day but can certainly make my patients feel better by ensuring they have everything they need both medically and materially, by getting the doctor's attention if their medications need to be changed, by letting their families know what's happening. One of the biggest things a nurse should do is act as a communicator, explaining doctors' instructions to patients and families. Importantly, you've got to keep a family informed about changes to the patient's condition. They shouldn't be taken by surprise, thinking everything is fine when actually their loved one's condition is heading south. As a geriatric nurse who has spent her entire career in skilled-nursing facilities, I've seen many people pass on. My first nursing instructor was right—you can't change rule number one, but you can help people be prepared for it.

Now, thirty-plus years into this career, I still come home at the end of the day and evaluate that day's performance by the act of looking my family in the eye. Though sometimes it makes me feel like a dork, I have to know in my heart that whatever I did out there in my nursing world, I did my best. That they would be proud of me.

That said, my dedication to ensuring other people's good health didn't necessarily apply to my own. Meaning, of course, that I continued to smoke. It was a deeply ingrained habit that I viewed as a personal choice. Even days when I'd be caring for someone with emphysema or lung cancer, the moment I took my break and went outside, those cases had no bearing on the Salem in my hand. In fact, the more that people told me I should quit, the more I wanted to go have a cigarette.

In my mid-twenties, I unfortunately developed a smoker's cough. Cold air would set me off, walking up a flight of stairs became difficult and was usually followed by some hacking. It didn't faze me though, I just kept on smoking.

While I was starting to show damage physically from my decades-long habit, psychologically I was doing much better. The antidepressants were doing their job and I was getting a lot better at working through the dread and panic. When I needed to get calm or just because I had some time, I would drive to the banks of the Mississippi River. Watching the water flow by, peering across the water to Illinois on the other side, it's one of the most peaceful places on the earth. The beautiful scenery, the golden yellows and orange browns calm me. I could spend a whole afternoon just watching the nature there. At the same time, I'm always aware that this peaceful scenic river has immense power. The Mississippi can be angry and powerful and create massive floods.

Sometimes I would think about how those rolling currents mirrored my emotional landscape. I was learning that some of my feelings could be similarly powerful. Pride in a job well done, sure. That was looking good. Satisfaction in having conquered my childhood demons, yes. I was immensely proud of that. The thing I couldn't shake, that could tank an entire weekend for me was the loneliness I felt. I'd see my siblings moving forward, getting married and having kids, and feel both happy for them and sorrow for myself. I so desperately wanted a child and a family of my own. My mom would always say "Lori, it's going to happen, and when it does it will be forever." I was beginning to doubt her wisdom.

Just after I turned 30, I moved into an apartment close to my work at a complex called Bogey Hills. It was just minutes from my job and was super convenient. Plus, it had a pool! One day I noticed a rather handsome man down there as I cut through the pool deck on my way to change into a suit. I was rubber-necking a bit too hard, though. Instead of watching where I was walking, I almost walked directly into the pool with all my clothes still on. I was so embarrassed and realized two things that day. Number one: I could never go to this pool again, and number two: this gorgeous man would never be mine.

One night after driving home from my shift, I stopped in the parking lot before going inside. The moon was waning and seemed to be calling to me. I looked up and wondered about a faceless man—a man who would love me, someone who would care for and support me and I could support him too. I wondered if he was looking up at the moon at that very moment too.

My sister Carol worked at True Manufacturing in O'Fallon, Missouri. She had been there for years. She made coolers for a living and she had a tightknit group of friends and acquaintances. A man named Mark worked right next to her. She knew about my loneliness (heck, she heard about it weekly), and decided she might just be able to play matchmaker. After thinking about it for a while, Carol decided to give Mark my number. "Give Lori a call, I think you two would make a cute couple."

There for a week or so Mark and I were just missing each other on the phone. I'd be busy at work or he would be busy doing his thing. This was pre-cell phones. In the nineties, you had an answering machine at home, and—imagine this—no one could reach you when you left for the day. Sometimes I miss that freedom of being able to just be in one place at a time. When you were at work, personal stuff just had to wait. When you were at home, you weren't required to communicate with work unless it was an emergency. Simpler times.

Finally, Mark and I caught up with one another. We made arrangements to meet up at my apartment to get to know one another.

The night he came over, I had set out some sodas and chips. Since I was working the overnight shift that night, we had to keep the beverages alcohol free. That shift starts at 10:30, but luckily a friend on the evening shift said she'd cover me until 11:30.

When Mark arrived looking extremely nervous, I knew he was taking this seriously. We had a fun time talking and asking all the usual questions.

"Do you have siblings?"

"What do you do when you're not working?"

"Oh! You love Dale Earnhardt?! Me too!" (Another racer in my life!)

Though technology has definitely changed, it's funny how the get-to-know-you rituals are still identical from generation to generation.

After two hours had gone by and we were still talking about music and sports, we realized both of us were starving. There was an Italian place close by, so we walked over and got a table. Over pizza, the hours ticked by while we shared stories and laughed about growing up in a small town.

We ended up going on many dates and started doing "what lovers do." It was so exciting to be exclusively dating someone I really, really liked—maybe even loved! Over the holidays, we introduced each other to our families. Mark's mother had died many years ago. He and his stepdad maintained a close relationship. It was so nice to see a family that was close. Mark has two sisters and three brothers, and at the time some of them were still teenagers. It was so nice to see how peaceful their home was. At my family home, there are so many people and so much drama. You can't gather dozens of strong personalities together without someone being mad at someone else. Not at Mark's house. It was a much more peaceful scene there, and Mark's strong, steadying presence was something that I could see they respected and appreciated.

At my house, the introduction was a bit more mixed. My mother was very kind and endearing. She'd fix dinner for us and try to make everything so welcoming and gracious.

Abraham was his flippant and negative self, as usual. "How much do you make at True?" he said in a sarcastic tone. I paid Abraham no mind. I was beginning to think this thing with Mark might just stick.

As the ball dropped on New Year's Eve that year, I had no idea how wonderful my 1998 was going to be.

Not long after the new year began, I noticed I was physically different. My breasts hurt. I was more tired than usual, and my period was late. It finally dawned on me. It couldn't be . . . I realized I could be pregnant. I'd been thinking that having missed my prime child-bearing years, I might not be able to have a child. Of course, this flash of insight happened when I was at work at 2:00 a.m. I was about ready to clock out for lunch, so I took the opportunity to run to the 24-hour grocery store and grab a pregnancy test. In the bathroom at work, I was both scared and excited. Standing there, waiting for a line to appear in a window, you get a chance to see what you're hoping for. I found that I really did hope for a positive test.

At that point, I was 33 years old. I had watched my brothers and sisters have babies for literally decades. As the plus sign became incontrovertible, I let out a sob of relief. Looking at myself in the mirror, tears streaming down my face, I smiled. I was pregnant!!! Finally.

When I went back to the patient floors there was a little pep in my step. I couldn't wait to tell Mark when he came over later that day. I was whistling and winking at everybody that night.

I woke up the next afternoon holding my stomach. Of course, I couldn't feel anything yet. I was maybe six weeks pregnant at that point. I think every woman does that—starts subconsciously protecting that little life inside. It was funny to me that even asleep, I was already pregnant in my mind. I had to get dressed, Mark was coming soon. I hadn't told anyone yet; I wanted Mark to be the first.

Mark came to the door and I let him in. I kissed him and hugged him and blurted it out.

"I'm pregnant."

I've never seen a grown man faint, but that's almost what he did right there in the kitchen. This Desert Storm army veteran who'd survived enemy attacks turned white as a sheet and sort of swayed and laid his head down on the counter. I had Mark sit down and got him a glass of water. Here we were again. Talking late into the night in my apartment, this time about our future together, about our baby. The next day, Mark skipped his usual routine of working overtime and returned to my apartment. "Lori, I just wanted to tell you, I'm all in." He was a man of few words, but I felt confident that he would be true to them.

I knew I needed to make a doctor's appointment right away to confirm the pregnancy. I got in at the OB-GYN right away and within the week, he confirmed that I was, indeed, pregnant. I started prenatal vitamins and made plans to tell my family.

I called my mom first. She couldn't hold in her excitement. "Oh, Lori! That's wonderful!" She was so happy for me. My dreams of being a mother were finally happening.

I then called my sister Carol. "Are you sitting down?" I asked her.

"Yes," she said.

"I'm pregnant!"

"Shit. Hold on, I wasn't sitting down." Carol laughed as I told her my story. She was so happy for me, as well. I left it to her to make sure everyone in the family got the news.

Mark and I settled into pregnant life, trying to eat the right things and trying to not smoke cigarettes. Though smoking had become such an ingrained part of my identity that I didn't stop for my own health, I had to do it for my baby. So I did. I'm proud to report that I was mostly successful.

One night I was at work and I reached across my desk and my belly touched the desk surface before I reached the stapler. That was the first indication that I was getting my baby bump. Some new moms have a bit of sadness about a growing belly, but not me. I was so overjoyed I couldn't hold back the tears and excitement. Picture me at my desk at the nurse's station in the nursing home at 3:00 a.m., holding a Swingline stapler and weeping with joy. It might have been the hormones, but I think it was mostly just joy.

Mark and I hadn't really settled on a boy's name, but if it was a girl Mark insisted her name would be Caitlen. I don't think I had a gender preference, just hoped for a healthy baby. Either way, it was an exciting time, especially since I was starting to feel flutters in my stomach. When it would happen, I'd imagine a palm-sized little person, kicking and doing flips in there. This baby was active and hopefully having fun in there.

We got to the medical offices feeling pretty nervous. The day had arrived when we would know the answer to the big question: was it a girl or was it a boy? The ultrasound jelly was cold on my tummy. Mark's eyes lit up when the heartbeat swished through the ultrasound speakers, a fast fuzzy beat, filtered through liquid and tissue. We both watched the screen as if our lives depended on it because, really, they did. The tech let out a breath and said those magic words, "It's a girl." We were so happy, crying tears of joy.

That Friday night, Mark and I were watching TV like we always did before I had to go to work. We were holding hands as usual. Mark said, "Lori, look at your hand." I looked down and there was an engagement ring on my finger. How did he get it there without my noticing? Again, tears of joy came streaming down my face. I, of course, said *Yes!*

Neither Mark nor I was very religious. Sure, I grew up Presbyterian, but I wasn't active in the church at that time, so it didn't feel important to me to go through the whole church wedding thing. We wanted to get married quickly and came up with some unconventional ideas. A Saturday afternoon wedding scenario was so expensive, and we were definitely on a strict budget. Instead, we elected to exchange our vows at the "chapel of love" in historic old town St. Charles, Missouri. It was a wedding business that shared a building with a plumbing store. When friends asked where we planned to marry, we'd joke that we were getting married at the "chapel of love and plumbing supply."

Our wedding was on March 27, 1998. I wore a beautiful white lace dress that I already owned, and Mark donned a new forest-green suit. We looked our best. We wanted to celebrate small and invited only select friends. Because it was a Friday, just a few family members were able to attend.

I thought about the traditional wedding rituals and decided that the best thing to do was walk myself down the aisle. Abraham was there but I didn't want him giving me away. That felt wrong to me. So, with my all-white orchid and rose bouquet, I marched myself down the aisle to Mark and the pastor. The officiant was a woman, and when I landed on my spot, she noticed that the entire bouquet was falling apart. My face must have shown some worry or fear—the arrangement had cost $200!

She said, "Oh my goodness, are we OK?"

"Yeah, we're fine. Let's get to it!" I said.

Because there was no entourage, no bridesmaids, no grooms-men, things went pretty quickly. We both said, "I do," and officially became Mr. and Mrs. Mark Tucker.

Now, twenty-two years later, I can say we're still best friends as well as husband and wife.

CHAPTER 9

Mark and I honeymooned in Kansas City, home to some of the best barbecue in the world. Happily, I was past the nauseous stage of pregnancy. The brisket, cornbread, and fries were some of the best I've ever had.

When we got back, of course we settled into married life in the apartment where I'd been living before.

We both worked. Mark was on days and I was on nights then, so we had our evenings together. Such is the life of a nurse. I've worked every shift—days, evenings, and nights—and don't really mind any of them. They all have their pluses and minuses; the biggest factor, of course, is the way your shift and your family time line up. I was grateful that Mark and I could continue our evening hangouts. We'd eat dinner/breakfast, watch a little TV, then I was off to the nursing home and Mark went off to bed.

With the wedding done, I was figuring the next big family event would be the birth of our daughter in the fall, but that was not to be. On May 20, 1998, I got a call at work at approximately 2:30 a.m. Abraham had had an episode and 911 had been called for him. I let my coworkers know that I had to leave; my mother needed me, and I left. I rushed home to let Mark know. By the time I got home, I received a second phone call. Abraham had died.

The sun hadn't even risen yet and my world had shifted dramatically. I'm not a monster, I did not jump up and down and say, "Yay! He's dead!" At the same time, I did feel relief. A weight had been lifted from my shoulders. From the second I heard that I was carrying a girl, I had felt a sense of vigilance was necessary. I'd vowed never to leave Caitlen alone in my mother's house.

After the second phone call, I breathed a sigh of relief while patting my tummy. I would never have to worry about Caitlen's safety with regard to the man who had hurt me.

Mark decided to stay home with me that day. We headed up to Elsberry to be with my mom. Once at the house, we learned that Abraham had experienced a massive heart attack. He was gone before the paramedics could get him to the hospital. We all sat at the kitchen table and discussed final arrangements. My mother was doing OK—visibly shaken, but OK. I spent that day and the next few at my mother's side, bringing her cups of coffee and talking her through the necessary steps of planning a funeral.

Family from California was coming in, so I picked them up at the airport. Aunt Trudy was there with her suitcase. In the car on the way back, she asked how the pregnancy was going. "I'm fine, just making sure my mom's OK."

"You're a dear," she said.

Everyone who knew Mom was worried about her. The whole town just loved her so much and wanted her to be cared for during this hard time. For the next two days, I remained at Mom's beck and call if she needed anything. The memory of my vow to protect my mom was still seared in my memory. I was her daughter; of course, I wouldn't be anywhere else.

There was a part of me that was, deep down, pretty relieved my mom no longer had to live with Abraham. Not that she was ever in any danger. She wasn't. But Abraham had grown into a bitter, angry man. It might have started around the time I stood up to him, but his pissed-off-at-the-world attitude had grown. Mom told me once about a time right after he retired that Abraham was outside trying to fix the fence and "had an anger episode." Apparently, it hadn't gone well because he was out there shouting and pounding on the wood as if to murder it. He can't have been easy to live with.

The wake was held on a clear Friday in late May at the funeral home in Elsberry. It was my birthday, but I wasn't mad about that. Everyone was telling stories about Abraham, remembering the times he had made them smile or laugh. I would occasionally join in and smile. Sometimes, when a difficult family member dies, their victims come unglued when the pressure is off to stay silent. I felt none of that. I was very relaxed. It was an end of an era for me. The second bogeyman was gone, and I felt relieved.

That summer, I felt wonderful. The baby was growing and kicking, which never failed to make me smile. I was still so happy to finally be having a baby. Everyone said I glowed.

My family threw a baby shower for me and I got a lot of nice things. I made sure that the first present I opened was the one from Mark. "Oooh," I breathed. In the box was a white blanket for our daughter with *Baby* printed on the front. That blanket would prove to be a very important lovey for Caitlen, made all the more special because it came from her dad.

It was a new experience for me, being the center of attention. Being the baby of the family, I had always sought the approval of my sisters and sister-in-law. They were older, and I had looked up to them and their experience as mothers. Now that I was finally reaching this milestone, I was really happy. And they were happy for me, which was heartwarming.

I was due in early September and by then, I was really feeling pregnant. Though I hadn't seen my feet for weeks, I was still working, tending my patients at the nursing home. They were excited for me and kept saying I'd better bring that baby to see them as soon as I could. Mark often joked, "Lori's going to have the baby on the weekend, so she doesn't miss work." That never failed to get a laugh.

The day before my due date, Mark and I decided we were going to barbecue for dinner. The moment we made that plan, I started feeling ill and my back began to hurt. Then I started having contractions. They weren't close together, so, first I called my mother. Yes, I'm a nurse, but not a labor and delivery nurse. Also, nurses need their moms too.

"Mom, I think I'm in labor."

Mom said, "Wonderful! How are you doing?"

"It hurts. I think these are contractions . . . in my back!"

"Well, it'll be OK. If they continue, go to the hospital."

Sure enough, I was having back labor and my contractions were getting closer together. Off we went to St. Luke's Hospital in St. Louis, an hour away.

I arrived at the hospital's emergency room where they immediately took me to labor and delivery. They hooked me up to IVs and monitors and I could hear my baby's heartbeat in the room. I was apprehensive about what would happen but felt confident that this was a healthy strong baby and things would turn out fine. Finally, after being an aunt for so long, it was going to be my turn!

The next several hours were spent breathing and pushing with Mark there holding my hand the whole time. First babies take forever, and this birth was no exception. I clearly remember the doctor saying, "She needs to have this baby soon." Mark looked worried and exhausted, but he was a calming, reassuring presence.

At exactly 7:00 a.m. that September morning, our adorable Caitlen was born. They immediately put her on my chest, and it was love at first sight. My sweet, sweet girl was here.

"Hello, baby," I said. I swore to protect her and love her for her whole life. She was my daughter.

I looked up to see Mark's reaction to this moment. I've seen Mark Tucker have a tear in his eyes only twice in my life. Once when Caitlen was born; the second was when Dale Earnhardt was killed. He was over-the-moon excited. There was a lot of love going on in that room.

My mother and Carol were outside in the waiting room. They joined our quiet family celebration. It was the best day ever, truly the happiest day of my life. Caitlen was here, she was fine, she was healthy. She weighed exactly seven pounds and, of course, we were all in love with her immediately.

I spent the next couple of days in the hospital. Mark was right by my side. We were able to bring her home with us on Monday;

Mark had taken the week off to give us three time to adjust to our new life. It's funny how a baby changes life in every aspect. We were proud parents and were just over-the-moon excited to have her home.

Mark was such a proud papa. He took to fatherhood like a dolphin to water. It was out of the norm for a midwestern man to dote so on an infant, but he didn't care one bit. He showed her off every chance he would get, grinning from ear to ear the whole time. The first trip Caitlen took was down to the Quick Trip, the convenience store where he'd worked. Mark wanted his friends who were still there to see what a marvelous little girl we had. I too loved showing friends and family my baby. I knew I was going to protect her—with my life if necessary—for as long as she lives.

That year the holidays came very quickly for us. Of course, we had Christmas pictures and "Baby's First Christmas" everything; I still hang all her ornaments on the Christmas tree. My first shopping excursion for Caitlen was quite comical. This being the first Christmas, it felt like a momentous occasion, so off to Toys R Us I went! I felt like I needed a bullhorn so I could clear the aisles: "FIRST TIME MOM HERE, PEOPLE, STEP ASIDE!" There was definitely a little pep in my step as I wheeled a cart full of newborn clothes, mobiles, stuffed animals, and whatever else I could grab that would catch her little eye.

Our family celebrates Christmas on Christmas Eve, we always have. That way Christmas Day can be set aside to play with toys, try on clothes, and unfortunately eat everything in sight. That year, we went to my mom's. She always made two big turkeys with all the fixin's to serve her giant family. Everyone came, and it was amazing to look around at the spectrum of faces there. All my brothers and sisters and their kids were there. Caitlen was grandchild number 51!!! A large family to say the least. Mom and Abraham had moved into a very nice large home in Elsberry but it still had a hard time holding all of us. We made the most of it and enjoyed everyone's company. It was Caitlen's first Christmas and she was the hit of the party. I walked around introducing the new family member. In a baby voice, I said, "Hi, I'm Caitlen. I'm new in town. Probably be seeing you around."

Everyone ooohed and awwwwed at her. My family loves a new baby, and Caitlen was no exception.

CHAPTER 10

While the rest of the world had started worrying about what would happen when the computers clicked down to the end of the year and that Prince song from the eighties was back in heavy rotation on the radio, for us, 1999 was about figuring out how to be a family. Mark and I were working our opposite shifts and loving on Caitlen as much as possible.

She was a great baby, smiling and taking in the world most of the time. She didn't cry a lot, she just seemed content most of the time. On Mother's Day that year, she had gotten a small cold, her first. I remember Mark picking her up to soothe the fussiness away. "It's about time you give me some trouble, young lady," he said, lifting her up on his shoulder to pat her back and kiss her downy head.

I delighted in witnessing all of Caitlen's firsts: those sharp little teeth cutting through her gums, first time crawling, first trip to the pumpkin patch where she rode a pony with Mark walking right next to her. Caitlen's first haircut was memorable; she didn't cry or fuss about having a stranger with scissors touching her head. I still have her baby hair in a special dish on my bedroom dresser. (Yes, I am a sentimental mother—no shame whatsoever.)

Since Mark and I felt so blessed to have this brown-eyed girl in our lives, we decided to just go all out on celebrations. For her first birthday, we rented a hall and invited everyone we knew. *Blues Clues* was her current fascination, so we got a large paw-print cake that was actually five cakes put together to form a paw print. We had a barbecue feast fit for kings and loved catching up with friends and family who traveled to be there. Just like the previous Christmas, Caitlen was the hit of the party. A lot of babies will get overtired and fussy in large crowds like that, especially when so many people are making a point to talk to them. Caitlen handled it calmly, smiling or gazing contentedly over the crowds through her great big brown eyes. She was just watching the show. When it came time for gifts, I was so honored to see the first card she opened had a $100 bill in it. It touched me that our family and friends were so generous and happy for our little family. Everyone knew how long I'd wanted a baby and they were happy for us. It was a good day for all.

The next few years were exactly the same as so many other families' day-to-day lives. We hired a daycare close to Mark's employer so Caitlen wouldn't have to stay but a couple of hours each day. I'd drop her off in the afternoon and head to my shift, Mark would be there just a few hours later, and everyone was happy for the time being.

Having worked as an LPN for over sixteen years, I had started to wonder about getting my registered nursing degree. Being a nurse isn't a job, it's a way of life. I was already all-in on this career and getting that degree would mean I'd be able to move into supervisory roles and, of course, receive more pay. Caitlen wasn't a baby any longer, and it felt like the right time. So, I enrolled at St. Charles County Community College for the two-year RN program.

Mark and my mother were so happy to see me returning to school. The first semester was good; I felt like a kid again doing homework and studying. It had been so long since I'd been in a classroom or had homework due! Mark helped me with my papers. I wasn't much of a typist. He was glad to help and I dictated what I wanted him to type. The second semester was harder. I had to take Algebra and realized that the general math course I'd had in high school did not put me at the same starting line that everyone else was at. The instructors were just assuming I knew about linear equations and solving for x. My school did not require that for graduation, so I'd had none of that at all. I felt like my childhood days of being bad at school were inserting themselves back into my adult life. There were tears. Mark tried to help me, but I had to come to terms with the fact I was not good at math and it showed.

During this time, I changed my hours at work so I could still be a full-time nurse, student, mother and wife. I went to school all day, then worked the 3:00 p.m. to 11:00 p.m. shift at the nursing home. Work was so understanding and allowed me to come in late and make up those hours on the days when my classes ran past my shift start time. I saw Caitlen and Mark on the weekends and slept whenever I could. Life was tricky. I had no idea that my life was going to take a sharp turn for the worse.

January 23, 2003 was just a day like any other day. I had finished up school and was at work that evening when I got a call from my mom. I picked it up on the wall phone in the common area that was the hub for all the nurses to communicate. Right next to that big desk was an aviary, a giant bird cage that the facility kept parakeets in so residents would have something joyful and beautiful to watch. I stared at a little green bird, its yellow head bobbing up and down, as my mom told me the worst thing possible.

"Lori, I have some news. My stomach hasn't been feeling right lately. So . . . I went to the doctor last week. I got some test results back today."

Through blood tests and ultrasounds, they detected a large mass on her liver. A biopsy showed that Mom had liver bile-duct cancer. That had spread to her breasts. She went all the way through those diagnostic tests without telling anyone because she didn't want us to be worried until there was a good reason to be worried. That was how she was, taking care of everyone in her own way.

I was in shock. I dropped the phone, went to the bathroom and threw up. On the way to my boss's office, I called Mom back to tell her I was on my way. Sitting in the old, plastic chair in the supervising nurse's office, I broke down as I told her my mom had cancer. A kind woman, and a veteran nurse, she was deeply sympathetic. She could see I was in no shape to drive, so she called Mark to come get me. He came right away, and we gathered a few things, our sweet baby, and hit the road to Elsberry.

At Mom's house, some of my brothers and sisters were already there. We all hugged and surrounded my mom. She said she had one more call to make and that was to Ted. She'd saved that one till last, knowing he would take it the hardest. Her voice broke several times during the conversation; it was hard to watch her accept this new role—the person who needed care instead of caretaker.

Mom was always the person who organized the family fun, be it baseball tickets or giant Christmas Eve feasts. She was the person who stepped in to help community members in need of support. Any time a local club needed catering for an event, Mom would break away from working at Red's and go all out making their food. No matter the time of year, she always made a Thanksgiving turkey with all the sides. I don't think there was an adult in Elsberry that hadn't loved and appreciated Mom's turkey dinner at some point or another. Between all those local friends and her children, Mom had an amazing support system. Together, we were ready to face cancer head on.

I hadn't forgotten that promise I made to my mom when I was five years old. I would always protect her, and I wasn't stopping now. All her doctors' appointments were set up so that one or more of us could go with her. I made sure I was there even if it meant to just hold her hand.

My mother never really had a positive doctor appointment. Today, there are infusions and targeted radiation that could help, but for Mom there was no talk of battling back the cancer. Oncologists, gastroenterologists, and general practitioners all used hushed tones when talking about her terminal diagnosis. Every one of them told us to appreciate this sweet, sweet time we had left. They estimated she had between six and eight months left to live. I was devastated.

One thing those conversations about time made me realize was that I didn't have any hours available to be in a classroom right then. I still had to work, but I did not have to be in school—didn't want to be in school—not when my mom had months to live. I wanted to spend them with her. It was hard because I knew I risked not going back, but I decided to put nursing school on the back burner. I'd get back to my RN degree when I could.

Decision made, my days were much freer. Instead of daycare and college, Caitlen and I drove to Elsberry every day to hang out with Mom/Grandma till I had to go to work at 3:00 p.m. Mom didn't like the fact I put school on the back burner, but I had no choice.

Early on, Mom, Caitlen, and I would go to lunch. She loved Mexican food and always ordered enchiladas, though she could make pretty good ones at home. I can remember sitting there in the restaurant, Caitlen munching on a cheese quesadilla, and laughing about whose enchilada sauce was better, hers or mine.

I'm glad I took that time to be there. My mother and I had a lot of private conversations. Most were about Caitlen growing up. I can remember sitting in her kitchen, summer light filtering through the curtains. The tears dripped off my nose as she told me that I was a "fine mom, one of the best I've ever seen." It's a jewel I still cling to today. I valued her opinion and hung on every word she said, sealing them in my memory forever.

Over the summer, we flew to California for Mom to visit her sisters. There was lots of laughing and crying. I hated the crying. It was a hateful reminder that I wasn't going to be able to protect her from this. I was so scared for my mom and me. She was supposed to help me watch Caitlen grow up to be a young lady. She was supposed to help me with her wedding. This was not fair. God was not fair.

On one of our trips to California, I remember Mom standing on the beach looking out at the Pacific, singing, holding her
hands together in front of her abdomen. I wondered what she was
thinking about, but I never asked her. It occurred to me then that
I needed to memorize these details so I'd always have them.

I started trying to keep track of every moment I had with Mom.
How she held her hands in her lap at the kitchen table where we
spent hours and hours drinking coffee, talking, and smoking. Mom
would wave her hands to make a point, her perfectly manicured
nails looking so beautiful. Mom loved wearing rings; in addition
to her wedding set, she had a ring set with nine small diamonds
that she wore on her right hand. Those hands that stuffed so many
turkeys and rolled so many pie crusts, they held so much love.

My mom's sister, Trudy, came out from California a couple
of times, as well. It was bittersweet. Everyone was happy she was
there, but there was an unspoken sorrow in the air. Most of the
time we liked to keep things lighthearted, but everyone knew why
she was there.

Summer turned to fall, and we still had Mom, but conversations with her doctors turned to questions about her comfort.

"How are you, Carol?" they would ask. "Are you in any pain?"

She did have pain in her abdomen that she tried to hide at first.
She was bloated, she said it felt like severe indigestion. Finally, it
got to be too much, and Mom admitted that she needed something to help her cope. We picked up the pain medication on the
way home.

It was tricky to be on the patient side of the room. Not tricky
because of the medical staff, tricky because my siblings still saw me

as the baby of the family. I'd been in nursing for twenty years by then, specializing in end-of-life care, but unfortunately the oldest siblings had been in charge of everything forever and didn't want my opinion—even when I knew more on the topic. It kind of hurt my feelings, to be honest. I could see that Mom's blood pressure medications were no longer necessary. Her readings were running low, not high. Those recommendations were dismissed. They thought I was too blunt because I kept asking Mom questions about end-of-life decisions. At work, I have these conversations daily, and families appreciate the direct approach. They need to be kept up to date with the changes so they're not caught off guard. There at Mom's house, that matter-of-fact bedside manner was coming off as pushy and unwelcome.

As the months went on, I noticed that if Mom was in the sunlight, she looked yellow. Her liver was failing. Human bodies are amazing. They have a whole bunch of toxic substances inside, but when functioning correctly, the liver and kidneys filter them all out. That system makes a person who they are: a functioning adult. When those don't work correctly, confusion goes through the roof, the patient gets very tired and weak, they're no longer able to function at the same level.

Watching this process I knew so well happen in my own mother—yet having my hands tied by birth order—left me feeling helpless. Mom grew more tired as the weeks went on, though the large family gatherings continued. At a certain point, the confusion and weakness were apparent to everyone, which was when we decided as a family to call hospice. With her weakened condition she required extra help moving about, and we were all happy to help. We had made a promise to Mom that when it came to the point where she couldn't do her regular routine on her own, we would keep her at home. She didn't want to leave her home, so we all took turns being there for her with the help from the hospice workers. We used a local hospice company with awesome nurses who came in to help Mom. They were full of good information and always treated Mom with care, comfort, and understanding.

Due to her rapidly decreasing mobility, a hospital bed was brought in so she didn't have to attempt stairs any longer. They placed it right next to Mom's favorite window in a sitting room where she loved watching the birds. Abraham and Mom's home was located out in the country, alone in the middle of this beautiful, lush valley. Through that window, Mom watched the greens shift to yellows, browns, and oranges. The grasses were drying and the trees were letting go of the season.

During these months, Mark and I had had a house built in Troy, just half an hour away. It was a little three-bedroom house that we'd had painted blue, in a suburban neighborhood. Compared to Mom's house, it was small, but it was ours to raise Caitlen in and we were very proud of it. Mom was able to come see our new home when it was completed in November 2003. I remember stopping on the way in the kitchen door to tie Mom's shoe for her. She looked exhausted by the trip, but she had wanted to come and see. She loved watching her children do well for themselves.

"I'm so proud of you two," she said. Even though she was smiling through some pain, I could see it made her happy to see her youngest child thriving.

The 2003 holiday season was met with mixed emotions. I loved the holidays but knew this would be the last one spent with my mom. That Christmas Eve my sisters cooked. The weather was bad, it was snowing hard. I was in Troy waiting for Mark to get off work. He made it home but even he—master of ice and snow driving—was questioning the weather. It was still snowing heavily.

"Lori, I don't know. It's bad out there. I heard we might get seven inches."

"Mark, this is Mom's last Christmas! I can't miss it. We have to get there somehow."

So, we checked that the SUV had a broom, a scraper, and our coats. We got Caitlen secured in her booster seat and headed to Elsberry. We took it easy speed-wise and made it there without incident. Looking around the house as I shook the snow off my hat, I saw that some of my brothers and sisters had gotten snowed out. I was glad we could be there so my mom wouldn't be alone. I settled in and sat next to Mother for the evening. We ate the turkey my sisters had prepared, with Mom, of course, at the head of the table. Afterwards, we turned on *Miracle on 34th Street* to fill the sad spaces in a bit. I watched Mom's every move closely. She was having bouts of confusion at this point.

"Did we eat dinner?" she'd ask.

I'd just nod and explain.

She would look at the Christmas tree, "That's so beautiful."

All of us knew this would be the last Christmas. We did our best to keep our happy faces on for Mom, then go to a different part of the house if we couldn't help but cry.

Caitlen was a trooper through this whole process; by now she was four. She only got upset if she saw me get upset. Then she would cry too, so I tried to keep up a brave face. The next few days were bad. Mom was getting worse by the minute and it seemed hospice nurses were in every day to see her.

January 4, 2004 is a day I will never forget. That was the day my mom died. There were several of us surrounding her bed as she took her last breath. I noticed no one was holding her left hand. I grabbed it, and we all did what we had been dreading for months; we held her hands and said goodbye. We all began sobbing. Cancer won.

There were so many people at her wake and funeral. Wall-to-wall people came to pay their last respects. The flowers were beautiful; her favorite flower, the yellow rose, was very well represented. The service was beautiful. So many people came to show respect for Mom. On the way to the cemetery, Mark and I were in one of the first cars. I looked back to see if everyone was following and gasped. As far as we could see, the road was filled with cars all lined up for Carolita May Price's funeral procession.

Mom left us one last act of service. After her death, we siblings all gathered at the funeral home to make arrangements. We knew funerals were quite expensive, so we'd all brought our checkbooks to pool resources.

"There's no charge," the director said, when he consulted his records. "Carol pre-paid for this service last spring."

We were shocked and humbled. Here was Mom, again, figuring things out on her own, taking care of her children.

CHAPTER 11

Days flowed past, and each one that would dawn, I'd have to remember again that Mom was gone. It was hard to remember, sometimes. When a milestone happened, like Caitlen's first day of kindergarten, I'd reach for the phone to tell her all about it. Then, just as quickly, my smile would fade with the sudden brutal reality that I couldn't talk to my mom ever again.

All those years of protecting Mom, of being her companion and helper, had left a deep imprint on me. I had worried about Mom's death—remember I worry about everything—but I'd never stopped to consider what life might actually be like without her. Let me tell you, it was bleak. Though, of course, my daily routines still had smiles and joy. I still went to work every day and enjoyed creating safe and caring spaces for residents with my work family. And Mark and Caitlen were absolutely the joys in my life. I'd go around filled with sorrow and joy or contentment, the grief just walking along beside me most of the time.

As most parents do, when Caitlen was little, we asked her what she wanted to be when she grew up. One day I asked that question and Caitlen answered, "A doctor!" I straightened up a little taller, feeling proud that my medical career was having an influence on my child. I could see her in a white coat with a wise expression on her face someday in the future. That feeling lasted about a day, when I asked her again, this time in front of Mark.

"Caitlen, tell Daddy what you want to be when you grow up!" I said, big old smile of expectation on my face.

"A monkey!" Caitlen exclaimed.

"Oh," I said, remembering that she was, after all, still just a little kid.

Caitlen was a firecracker as a small child. I can remember when I'd be trying to catch up on some sleep after a double shift on a Saturday morning, and she'd come running into the bedroom. Jumping up on the bed, her knees right next to my face, she'd scream in my ear, "Mommy! I want EEEEGGS!"

This happened more than once (and I noticed she never did that to Mark), but I would roll myself off the mattress, somehow walk into the kitchen, and scramble some eggs for my girl. Because that's how the life of a nurse goes. Your days often don't line up with the rest of the world's, but you just keep going somehow because you have to.

I longed to tell my own mom about the eggs and the monkey and all the events of my daughter's life. There was so much joy and pride in those years. Yet, there was a mom-sized hole in my heart that I felt constantly.

Psychologically I still dealt with panic attacks and depression that had continued to be treated throughout my life, but they remained stable even after Mom's death. I think that, on some level, I had come to expect tragedy. It was just one more thing I had to take like all the other events of my life.

One way I coped was the same way my mother had. I smoked. By now, I'd switched from Salems to Marlboros and was deeply committed to the habit. Even though I had developed a smoker's cough, I didn't want to stop. It was my thing, my way of finding peace and quiet in my mind and body.

Caitlen hated it because I always smelled like cigarettes. I can remember arguments with Caitlen as she got older and more socially aware. She detested the smell of the cigarettes and the way the smoke permeated her clothes and hair. By age 10, she was telling me, "Mom! You're making me stink too!"

By the time she was 12, I'd say, "Go ahead and get some of that body spray," handing her some money. Caitlen probably had hundreds of dollars' worth of perfume and scents for masking the smoke smell.

My daughter's disapproval didn't really faze me. Smoking was how I got through the day, how I managed to keep going on so little sleep. It was also a series of mini rewards that I allowed myself when I did chores. It was how I clocked my day: a smoke to wake up, a smoke after doing the breakfast dishes, a smoke on the way to work, a smoke on my first break, two smokes on my lunch break, etc. All that added up to two packs per day.

I didn't even quit when Mark had double pneumonia and had to stop smoking, which I still feel bad about. At the time, I was really ambivalent about his stopping because I wasn't ready to do so myself. I smoked all over the house, including in the bedroom, not taking his physical and mental health into consideration. It was the wrong thing to do, I know that now. At the time, I couldn't really face that I needed to make a change.

The health risks of smoking didn't really sink in until my sister Carol was diagnosed with a heart condition that landed her in Barnes Hospital in St. Louis, in the ICU. I remember going to visit her and seeing all these IVs, catheters, and tubes all over her, even in her neck. I looked at her bruised arms from all the veins they had already used and felt so sorry for her. This woman, my sister who practically raised me, who had tolerated my tagging along on her entire childhood, was hurting so badly. She couldn't catch her breath. She couldn't really talk without coughing fits.

As I stood there on the cold linoleum tile at the foot of Carol's hospital bed, I thought about the number of years she had smoked. All those afternoons at Mommy's kitchen table where we'd all shared an ashtray had come back to claim a price.

While we talked and laughed (gently), I started to feel scared that I'd lose her too. My second mother was so sick. I visited with her as long as I could that day. When I left the room, I looked back at her and saw not Carol Jean, but myself a few short years from now. If I didn't stop smoking immediately, I'd be the one in the hospital bed with oxygen cannulas up my nose and IVs in my arm.

The vision shook me up. By the time I got on the elevator and made my way to my car in the parking garage, I was starting to re-think my commitment to the Marlboro company. On the ride down to Level 2, I noticed the flutter in my lungs. At this point, I was either coughing or catching my breath from coughing. *I wonder what it's like to take a free breath?* I had reached my SUV. Standing by the driver door, I reached for my cigarettes and lit one up. I smoked exactly half of it while reveling in the calmness that washed over my body, worrying about what would happen to my anxiety without this crutch I'd been leaning on.

Then, I just threw my pack of cigarettes on the ground, placed my lighter with it, and drove away. I was tired of coughing all the time. I didn't want to end up in this same hospital, like my sister. I had to make a change.

That moment I pulled out of the hospital parking garage my life changed forever. I drove immediately to the grocery store and picked up the NicoDerm CQ patch. Sitting in the car, I pulled a patch out of the box right there in the store parking lot. Pasting it to my bicep, I then closed my eyes and started concentrating on my breathing, concentrating on the wheezing in my lungs. I thought *This is the worst I'm going to breathe. This is the worst I'm going to feel. It's going to get better from here. I have to make this work.* I had every confidence in the patch, knowing it would help me quit.

I got home and shared the news with Mark and Caitlen. "I did it, guys! I quit smoking!" This had never happened before, and my little family was understandably skeptical. The look they shared had a, *yeah, we'll see how long this lasts* in it. But I was finally motivated. Hellbent on change, I threw out all the ashtrays and the cigarettes. We didn't need those anymore. I gave all the lighters and matches to Mark for safekeeping.

I showed Mark the patches. "I'm really going to do it, but I'm scared about mornings." That first morning cigarette that every smoker loves was going to be hard to skip. Much like the first sip of coffee, it's a rush of stimulant through an empty system, and it feels oh so good. I knew missing that morning ritual would be my weakest time of day.

"Well," Mark said, "how about this? Since I get up before you, I can reapply your patch while you're still asleep. Then you won't wake up feeling low and wanting a cigarette!"

"You'd do that?"

"Of course, honey."

For this reason and so many others, my love for this man is immeasurable.

That first night, I remember lying down and, again, listening to myself breathe. It brought back a memory of the deep breathing I'd learned from the psychiatrists at the hospital. But since those years in my early twenties, I had smoked almost half a million more cigarettes. Literally, I had smoked 408,800 cigarettes owing to my two-pack-a-day habit for more than twenty-eight years. My lungs had a wheezy flutter in them all the time now. A full breath usually triggered a coughing fit. I pulled air in and waited for the spasms. Afterward, trying to quiet my breathing, I closed my eyes and again said, "This is the worst I'm going to feel."

The next few days were hard, but doable. The patch was doing its job and working tremendously well. My anxiety had always been bad, and for a while it would spike at the times when I used to smoke. I learned that if I focused on the craving, it could take over my entire heart, brain, and soul. I had to force myself to move forward without thinking too hard about it. I had the patch, my body still had the nicotine it was craving, albeit less and less of it.

Without the physical cigarettes, I had to find another way to move through my day. Unfortunately, some of the mini rewards got replaced with food. I reasoned that an extra twenty pounds was better for me than a deadly cigarette—and it was. But I also realized that I didn't need all those pit stops. I figured out that if I could just go do the dishes (or drive to work or pay the bills) without thinking I needed a cigarette, I would be successful. I just made my body do the task and the cravings passed after a couple of minutes. Ten minutes into the task, I'd look up and realize I'd made it through another craving. A reward in itself! Changing my habits around smoking was much harder than detoxing from the nicotine.

If I can pass on this wisdom to the world about not smoking, it would be smoking is a very personal thing. You can't force someone else to quit. The more someone told me not to smoke the more I wanted to smoke. The way I got out of it was realizing for myself that I was going to kill myself with the habit. Enough was enough! That, plus the support of my family, made it possible to quit.

Folks, it has been eight years since that last cigarette in the parking garage. I no longer wheeze or cough, but I remember all too well how I felt. I can actually walk up stairs without coughing! I get fewer colds, and best of all, my chances of developing heart disease have been cut in half. For me, I know one cigarette equals my death—an agonizing, painful death.

These days, when I mention it to new acquaintances, they can't believe I ever smoked. I always say, "I smoked for thirty years. The patch saved my life," and I really mean it.

I really am grateful to the makers of the NicoDerm CQ patch. That product got Caitlen her mom back, my husband his wife back, and me my life back.

CHAPTER 12

The next few years were spent simply watching my daughter grow into a beautiful, kind woman, tenacious to the core, mindful of her parents, a good friend to her peers, and a joy to be around. It was very important to me that Caitlen experience none of my childhood traumas. Mark and I both made sure that she was never in a situation that would be unsafe. But, at the same time, we wanted to let her spread her wings and not be so tied down to one place. She did that and so much more.

I remember Caitlen came home from school one day, age 16, all revved up about something. "Mom! I want to be in the travel club. They go all over the world."

"Uh . . . how much, honey?"

She told me and my stomach dropped. "I don't have the money to come up with the payments for that."

"If I get a job, can I pay for it?"

Stupid me said yes.

The next day she had a job at a local restaurant, working double shifts when she could, and started earning money towards her trip. There she was, wearing a uniform and slinging grilled cheese—exactly like I was at that age. God, her work ethic feels so familiar.

She held that job at the restaurant for three years, and with her earnings took two round-the-world trips and only called in sick at work once. She's been to Switzerland, all over Europe, to Australia . . . I'm so proud of her. She had a problem, found the solution, and went to some spectacular places at 18 years old! Back when I was 18, getting to St. Charles County was a stretch for me.

It was scary as a mom to see my baby go so far away. Of course, my anxious brain was thinking through all the possible pitfalls that might happen. I made Mark get his passport on the off chance that he'd have to fly out of the country to help her or get her if she got sick.

Caitlen graduated from Troy Buchanan High School in 2017. She was voted most likely to see the world. I'm enjoying her travels vicariously, though I just started the process of getting my own passport. I may just join her on a trip someday.

After high school, Caitlen enrolled at Johnson & Wales University where she was awarded a $60,000 scholarship. As a freshman, she declared a marketing major, which she had been planning for since high school. Though, she also said in the same sentence that if that didn't work out, she'd like to be a butcher. It made me laugh and remember the time she couldn't decide between doctor or monkey.

Dropping her off that first time, I was a mess. I was helping set up her bedding and desk lamp with my lower lip quivering the whole time. Caitlen has always picked up my feelings, so rather than have both of us sit there crying, she threw me out of the dorm. "Mom! Just wait outside. Dad can do it." I couldn't help it. I was going to miss her so much. I cried in the parking lot, and on the plane ride home. I think she missed me too since she's a frequent flyer on Southwest Airlines now.

There is one more person I need to introduce to my readers who is not a person at all . . . he's Henry!!! The most lovable, the most reliable, the best protector of all is our 115-pound German Shepherd. He was a Christmas Eve surprise for Caitlen when he was eight weeks old.

When Caitlen was about 16, she started talking about wanting a dog, and not just any dog, a German Shepherd. Up till now, we'd only had cats, so I was a little unsure at first. Her interest didn't waver at all. "Mom, please can we get a dog? It should be a German Shepherd and we should call him Henry." I started warming up to the idea that maybe a dog could be fun. With the help of my co-worker, Jennifer, I located a breeder in southern Missouri who had a litter coming right before Christmas. When he was eight weeks old, I told Caitlen I was going shopping and took off.

This daughter of mine is very protective of me. If I'm at work, she's fine, not worried at all. Anywhere else, she wants to know exactly what's happening and when I'll be back. So, being off the grid for a day resulted in quite a few calls from Caitlen wondering, where was I? What was I doing? She pestered Mark, as well, who only smiled and said, "She's shopping, babe." It was technically true, just not in the way she envisioned.

Back in town now, our new German Shepherd puppy hung out with Jennifer for the night while I tried not to smile too big.

The next day was Christmas Eve. Mark told Caitlen to get her shoes on. "Let's go see if that kitten we saw at PetSmart is still there. Maybe we should get him for Christmas!"

Caitlen was game, but when we walked through the front door of the store, there stood Jennifer, holding a wriggling ball of gray and brown fluff with ears. We had gotten him a bone-decorated collar with a monogrammed tag. *Henry*, it read.

"Ooooohhh!" Caitlen squealed and ran over to Jennifer. She took that puppy in her arms and just started bawling. "He's ours?"

"Yes, he is," we said, thrilled to be able to bring so much joy to our child's face.

Henry is five now and finally settled down, but that dog had a "ruff, ruff" puppyhood. Having such a quiet and reserved daughter, I was very surprised by how much mess and ruckus a dog could make. I would come home from an errand to find that he'd chewed the corner off the couch, or destroyed an entire package of toilet paper, or snatched the thawing meat off the counter. The wooden banister will never be the same, and the poor mailman is a very tolerant guy, but I suspect he's not a Henry fan. Some of that naughty behavior was our fault. We'd never had a dog before and didn't realize that German Shepherds, in particular, need a lot of structure. With the help of a trainer at the store, we were on our way to having a better relationship with Henry.

Today, he's just one of the family, though he still barks his head off at the mailman. And leaving the house usually costs me a couple of dog cookies to get my shoes back from Henry, who grabs them and holds them hostage the second he notices me getting ready.

Mark and I have a California king-size bed. Mark has a small portion, I get a small portion, and Henry gets the rest. I guess this is how it works for most dog lovers. He sleeps with me every night, always making sure his paw or some part of his body is touching me. He's my protector. Henry is one of the great loves of our lives. If you could give your dog an illness by petting them too much, I'm sure Henry would have it.

By 2019, Caitlen was halfway through with college, Mark and I were starting to settle into life as empty-nesters, and just working on our retirement fund, when things started to fall apart again. I had thought that life was settled and free from tragedy and chaos. I was wrong.

I'm sure people have experienced bad years during their life—2019 proved to be mine. First, my beloved brother was diagnosed with cancer. It was advanced and would take a lot of medical treatment, prayers, and love to help combat it.

That same spring, Mark and I started noticing a lot of standing water in the yard outside our house. We couldn't figure out where it was coming from. It was like living next to a creek. We could even hear bullfrogs in the backyard! We tested the sprinkler system, checked the water and sewer connections . . . finally, we had the city of Troy come out to investigate. Their conclusion? We had an underground spring in our yard. WHAT!?!

"How are we going to fix that?" we wondered.

We thought about it and were completely dumbfounded. Would we have to move? Would the value of the house completely crumble?

Then, of course, our basement started leaking. I was downstairs doing laundry, and I noticed cracks in the wall. Oh my gosh! The house was imploding! I envisioned waterfalls running through the basement, which was thankfully unfinished in the part that started leaking. But cracks in the foundation can mean the whole structure is suspect.

We didn't have any choice; we had the city come back out. This time, they looked a little harder, I guess. After some investigating, they noticed that the water seemed to be coming from above. Oohh, this was no spring. It was a leak! They started shutting off my neighbors' water supply. One house at the top of the hill still had water after the shutoff. The source of our Water-pocalypse had been found!

The leak was fixed quickly. What we needed to do now was let it dry out. Since we were essentially living in the middle of a lake, it was a bit of a waiting game. Though we were running industrial fans and wet/dry vacs for weeks, we didn't sue our neighbors. The thought was there but after seeking counsel, the lawyer said it would be too expensive to take them to court. Mark agreed, plus it's hard to live next to someone you have sued.

Instead of giving our money to lawyers, we found a local contractor and gave it to him in exchange for three enormous pits in the yard in which he installed supporting pipes. We added a second sump pump, and the house was deemed sound and safe. Now we just had to keep this from ever happening again.

Mark and I joked that we'd always wanted to have fancy landscaping installed in our yard. We weren't thinking we would be forced to have it done. But once the ground dried out, we had a beautiful wall and trees planted in the back of the house, with a unique drainage system installed that rerouted any rain or run-off around the house rather than to the house.

Between the yard and the basement, our cost was about $22,000. Ack. I work a lot of doubles anyway because life with a college student is expensive. I just added it to the list.

If those two disasters had been the only problems of 2019, that would have been enough. But my year of earth-shattering news was just getting started.

CHAPTER 13

The fall of 2019, Caitlen started asking more often about her heritage. I knew my mother was of Mexican descent with relatives in southern California. My father, Gene, was a red-headed Irishman. But, since our flight from his house when I was four, we had not been in touch. His death didn't bring any relatives in touch with us, so I knew little about his side of the family.

I guess those find-your-ancestors TV ads were starting to work on my daughter. She wanted to know if there were any royalty in our way-back family genealogy, or if she should be looking out for any genetic medical problems. Figuring it might be fun to see where the search went, I ordered her a 23andMe kit as a Christmas present. It was the best and worst $70 I've ever spent. Caitlen filled the test tube with saliva and sent it off, full of high hopes. Thinking of those craft and science kits I bought her when she was little, I actually thought *This will be fun for her.* Little did I know my life would crash down around me because of what we found.

After a few weeks, the results were in. I was heading out the door to run errands when Caitlen said, "Mom, I got the 23andMe back." I was thinking about snow tires and dog food and sort of just nodded.

"That's great, honey," I said, looking for my shoes.

"It says I have relatives in southern California."

"Well, sure. You know Aunt Trudy and her husband."

"Mom. No. It's beyond that." Her grave tone made me stop in my tracks and pay attention. "I don't just have cousins in California. It says I have a grandfather there."

"Huh? That's impossible." I sat down on the couch, errands forgotten. Gene was dead and Mark's dad had also passed away. By that point, all of Caitlen's grandparents were gone. This had to be wrong. The DNA results showed she shared three identical strands with another donor in their database, making her granddaughter to a man currently living in California. I was stunned, figuring it was some sort of error. Deep down, though, a part of me that had been put to rest started stirring again.

Over the next few weeks, Caitlen started receiving emails from the man in California, asking the same questions we were asking. "Who are your mother and father? What are their birthdates?" He introduced himself as Jerry. (For his privacy, only his first name will be used in this book.)

He sent a baby picture to Caitlen, asking if it was me. It wasn't, but because of the number of questions and the mystified way they were asked, it was becoming apparent that Jerry wasn't actually Jerry. Weeks went by and emails were exchanged. Eventually we found out we had actually been talking to Jerry's daughter posing as her dad. I guess she had done the same thing in sending off her own DNA test kit. Imagine how surprised she was when 23andMe notified her of a niece that no one knew about.

Through these email exchanges, Caitlen was doing all the talking. I decided not to join the conversation because I didn't know what to say. Officially I had no comment. I didn't know how to act. I had been completely blindsided by this news and just felt dumbfounded. How could it be that my mother had had an affair? Had she known Gene wasn't my dad? Was it possible that this was all some cruel joke or a terrible mistake? The feelings of panic and despair and tragedy that had permeated my childhood came back. In my adult life, I had really reached a place of peace and didn't struggle so much with my mental health. But now, it was like I was a child again, living under the same roof with a predator.

The following spring, my family had planned a big reunion. All the cousins, aunts, and uncles on my mom's side of the family met at a park near Troy, Missouri. My family flew in from California. This was meant to be a happy time, which it was. I looked around at the generations of family. There were heaps of fried chicken and potato salad, hot dogs, sodas, beers . . . all the ingredients for a festive family day. Little kids kept running back and forth between the potato chips and the playground, elderly aunts sat in the shade enjoying everyone . . . I looked at everyone there, all a part of this big family. None of them knew I had a big secret.

My emotions got the most of me and I sat down next to my cousin Terry, Trudy's daughter, and blurted out the words I had been trying to keep in for weeks.

"Hey, Lori, how you doing?"

"Apparently my mother had an affair, and I was the result of that affair!" Poor Terry looked understandably shocked. But now that I had started, I couldn't stop.

"Would you ask your mom if she remembers a man by the name of Jerry in my mom's life?"

"Uh . . . what's going on, Lori??"

I was so distraught I didn't care who heard me. I noticed a few relatives looking at me as I cried and talked, but they never approached me about it. I'm thankful for that. I also feel like I should publicly apologize to my cousin, Terry, for putting her on the spot like that.

The next days were spent going over and over the problem in my mind. *Why wouldn't Mom have said anything? Did she even know?* No one wants to consider their parents' sex lives, yet here I was wondering about my own mother's intimate partners. *Who is this man?* Yet again, I wished Mom was still alive, but for very different reasons now.

I decided I wanted to speak to Jerry personally. Since I couldn't ask my mother, I would have to talk to him. Caitlen relayed the message through his daughter that I had questions and gave him my phone number.

Throughout this time, I continued working. I'd been at work for most of the difficult things in my adult life and found that it was good for me to be in my natural element, serving my patients when my personal life was in disarray. I might not fill the same place in my family that I thought I had, but I still had my work family. Maybe I wasn't a full sister to Keri and Carol and my brother, but I was still an excellent nurse. I had a place in this world and people who relied on me.

I had just started a shift one afternoon when my phone rang. It was a number from southern California I didn't recognize. *It's him!* I thought and decided to take the call. I dropped into an empty room to get as much privacy as I could.

"Hello? Is this Caitlen?"

"No . . . it's Lori. Is this Jerry?"

"Oo-oh. Hi." His voice cracked a little when he realized it was me.

"Do you speak Spanish?"

What the. His accent indicated that English was his second language, and a whole other could-have-been life flitted before me. I thought about the number of times I had passed up opportunities to take Spanish in high school and college. It seemed like here was yet another family that I didn't quite fit into.

"I'm sorry to say I don't." We began talking about where he was from.

"I'm from east LA," he said. Jerry's accent reminded me a little of Tommy Chong from Cheech and Chong. I kept picturing this guy with an extra-long mustache and a headband talking to me and telling me about his life.

So many "what-ifs" stemmed from that conversation. What if I'd grown up with Jerry as my father? What if Mom had told me about him after she felt safe from Gene? Couldn't she at least have told me before she died?

I wasn't exactly longing for Jerry, though. The concept of fatherhood was such a complete misfire in my life. Gene had been bad, verging on evil. Abraham was worse. And now here was yet another not-quite father in my life who seemed OK, but who knew?

I told him that if he didn't want to talk to me again, I would understand, and I would be OK.

"Lori, I would never say that to you."

Wow. Unconditional acceptance after just one minute. Maybe this guy's OK.

Then, he said, "I've been married for fifty-two years. I hope after this conversation to still be married."

"...oh."

I realized at that moment that Jerry's wife was listening on the line. This revelation was news to Jerry's family too, I knew. I could feel from the pain and tension in his voice that his family was having a hard time. It's funny how much you can understand from things not said. I had become an expert in that art.

"How did you and my mom meet?"

"I was the mailman," he said.

My mind went blank like an emergency broadcasting system test . . . *THE MAILMAN!?*

Memories of my whole life raced through my mind. All those pancakes-and-eggs breakfasts where I was teased for being so much darker than the rest of them! All the times my siblings had joked I must be the mailman's kid and my mother just smiled like it was the funniest joke she'd heard all week. Why didn't she ever say anything? Didn't she realize how alone I had felt? How weird and ostracized I had felt? Was she laughing at me too all that time?

Jerry said that he and my mother had had an affair that lasted for about three months. I believe Jerry's wife was also pregnant when my mom was pregnant with me. When Jerry found out about me, Mom told him that Gene would probably kill him. Based on Gene's rages, she was probably right. The affair ended abruptly after that.

"I've been looking over my shoulder ever since," Jerry said.

"Well, you can stop worrying about that." I told him about Gene's death and about my mom's passing.

We ended our conversation, and I felt like I'd been shaken up like a snow globe. I was sobbing. Knees giving way, my body fell against the bathroom wall and I slid down it. Sitting on the tile floor, I flashed back on an entire lifetime of memories—memories that were now just slightly false. Was everything that I thought I knew a lie?

Mom, how could you do this to me? I loved her so much. I protected her my entire life. From age four, I had been her protector, her companion, her trusty daughter who tried to save her from bad men, who sucked it up and moved in with a new family, who endured the abuse from her second husband just so I wouldn't break the family apart. I was so loyal to her, and apparently, she didn't feel the same way.

My mind took me to a memory of Gene who I thought was my real father, shouting "I'm taking her to an orphanage tonight!" Why did he say that? Did he know? Is that why he held that gun to her head? As reality started sinking in, the orphanage seemed like it might have been better.

My mind turned to Abraham. Why did she expose me to him? He was a predator. I started counting up other ways Mom had failed me. She never told me that what happened with Abraham wasn't my fault—in fact we never talked about it at all. I was the one who was sent away, not Abraham.

At one point during those years of turmoil with Abraham, I remembered overhearing Mom outside talking to a friend. She sounded upset, so of course my ears tuned in to assess the threat. "Abraham thinks I'm having an affair." At the time, it seemed like a completely absurd idea. She wouldn't do that. I gave no credit to the theory and dismissed it out of hand. Now, I wondered.

The square yellow tiles on the floor swam in and out of focus as I dug through my perception of myself. Hard realities were sinking in. It seemed like my mom didn't love me quite as much as I'd loved her. If she had, she would have told me the truth at some point. She wouldn't have let me be the butt of the family joke about the mailman. I felt so foolish. The foundation I'd been standing on—the solid connection between a daughter and her mother—had just crumbled. I remember looking in the mirror and saying, "I am broken."

I left the bathroom a different person.

Still trying to find my footing in the world, I sat down at the nurse's station and placed a call to my sister, Carol. It wasn't pretty. I began shouting on the phone.

"Did you know I'm the product of an affair?!"

"What? Lori, you're not making sense." I explained what had just happened, how I'd just talked to my biological father and how he and Mom met.

"Mom must've thought I was some big joke, laughing while people called me the mailman's kid."

"Oh, Lori," Carol tried to be soothing, but I was enraged.

I hung up the phone knowing that Carol must have thought I was yelling at her. I wasn't angry with her, just at the way my life had come crashing down.

Why, oh why didn't Mom ever tell me? Once Gene was dead, there was no reason to hide any longer. We spent so much time together that year before her death. I rearranged my whole world to be there to care for her. Didn't she appreciate the loyalty? We had so many private conversations, and not once did she act like she wanted to say something but didn't. I had no idea she was holding anything back.

Though I had just lost my mind in a semi-public space, my co-workers made no comment about it. Either they didn't notice or pretended not to. I was grateful. I splashed cold water on my face in the bathroom, blew my nose, and got back to business. It was time for me to take care of my patients; my personal crisis could wait.

It was about dinner time and my people needed me to administer their medications and help them get fed. Wheeling residents to the dining room, no one was the wiser that my world had just shattered.

In the days that followed, Caitlen continued to back me one hundred percent, which I have always appreciated. Mark's first reaction was shock. Then he said, "Lori, it was her right not to tell you." Though Mark is my best friend and we can tell each other anything, this was not what I wanted to hear. My husband isn't the most comforting person in the world. After the smart wore off, I realized that he was right, of course. Mom had that right to keep a secret but look at the mess she made by doing so.

Sometimes families do keep secrets to try to avoid expanding a trauma. Yet somehow the suffering continues. Secrets cause a trauma of their own, and unfortunately, the results of Mom's secret have landed squarely on me.

Over the next few months, I tried to keep the story from spreading. The only two people I shared information with were my two sisters. My brother was fighting hard against cancer and it seemed unkind to burden him with this. I knew the story had leaked to other family members, but for now I continued to say I had no comment.

As the weeks went on, I was on the fence about telling my brother, Ted. He was a very sensitive person and could be very angry, especially with regard to our mom. Figuring that word was starting to travel, and it would be best if he heard about it from me, I gave him a call. My brother seemed to handle the conversation OK, though it started to get a bit heated after a few minutes. He was mad at me and trying to hurt my feelings.

"I guess you're happy now, you didn't like Dad anyway."

I shot back, "I was four years old, Ted. I didn't see your ass in the closet hiding from him when he was drunk."

When we hung up, I started worrying that my brother would carry this anger around, not the best thing for a person undergoing chemotherapy. I hoped he was going to be OK, but to ensure that he'd have someone to talk to about it, I called his daughter and retold the story.

I'm not sure what response I expected to get from my niece. It certainly wasn't, "Why did you have to tell him that? Why did you have to look that information up about Grandma?"

I was shocked at her anger. How could she think that of me? My relationship with my mother was so close. I couldn't ever imagine hurting her or my family. This was Mom's mistake, not mine.

Through Caitlen, I found out that the family was starting to talk on social media about this situation. Ted felt the same as his daughter, that I had no right to dig up Mom's past. It hurt my feelings to be talked about, especially in a public way.

I'm not on Facebook or Twitter or any of the social media platforms. Sometimes, friends and family question or pressure me about that decision. And sure, sometimes, it sounds fun to catch up with old friends and see their children grow up. Yet, I'm always aware that along with the reminiscing comes drama. So many arguments are had, so much gossip passed along . . . that's why I'm not there. But if I were, I know this story would be a heck of a controversy. If I had a Facebook page, this is what I'd post for any and all to see:

"I will say this one last time and then I will never talk about it again. The DNA search was an activity for Caitlen to get to know her ancestors. I did not intentionally try to dig things up about my mother, and, again, this was Mom's mistake. Not mine. No one caught on to her except technology. I bet she never thought DNA kits would ever be a thing."

Watching Caitlen serve as the go-between for me and my extended family has made me feel so sorry that I've put her in this position. My girl has hate in her heart and I never wanted that four-letter word to be a part of her life. She is so angry about how family members have received this news. The things they've said about me have festered inside her for most of a year, resulting in a scene about decorating this year's Christmas tree. "Don't put up your family ornaments, Mom. I don't even want to see those." She goes around ready for a shouting match with any member of the family who might have known my true identity. I hate that my Christmas present to her opened up this Pandora's box.

Though my inner cynic has grown very strong, I don't really think my family knew Mom's secret. Talking to Carol over coffee one day, she told me about a conversation she'd had with Mom one time. Somehow the topic of parents keeping secrets from their children had come up, perhaps it was a plot on a show they'd watched. Carol reported that Mom had said, "You make up your mind about what to say, and never stray from that."

It seems like Mom just decided that Gene was my dad and never revisited her relationship with Jerry, even in her mind. Aunt Trudy reported back through Cousin Terry that she had no idea her sister had found someone new, never heard anything about a Jerry. She also wondered if Mom's not telling me was for the best. Maybe I was better off not knowing, she said. I disagree.

As the months have passed, I have had a few occasions to talk to Jerry, and I've always found him to be kind. I wish I had known him when I was a child. He told me to not be mad about what Mom did. Even though this news has blown up his life, he's not bitter.

I feel so sorry for Jerry's wife. I don't even know her name, but if I could talk to her, I'd apologize for my mother's actions. Jerry told me that after the story broke, his wife wouldn't talk to him, cook for him, or do his laundry. His kids wouldn't talk to him, and only one grandchild would talk to him. I think his situation has improved, and this is why I'm not using his full name. His family needs a chance to heal. A part of me daydreams, sometimes. Of course, I would love to meet my biological father but not at the expense of his wife and family. This is not one of those happy re-unions you see on TV commercials, unfortunately.

If anyone in my family had a sense of something off, it was ac-tually my sister Keri. She never said a word about it until the truth emerged, but she told me afterward that she had always found it odd that I had AB+ blood. Keri and Ted are both O, an odd combination between siblings. I think of my sister as the problem-solver, the fact finder of the family. She's my Sherlock Holmes, which is why I took it to heart when she gave me some advice.

One day, I was worrying and raging over this issue with her. Keri said, "Lori, there's nothing or no one in this world that is ever going to make you feel any better about the situation." That comment stays with me 24/7. She meant it as a suggestion to go work out some of my anger in therapy—and I don't say this now to discourage anyone from seeking help; it's worked for me at other times—but I took Keri's words differently. For me, it seems like no amount of counseling is going to change the reality of this situa-tion. I've known this bizarre and utterly stunning fact about myself for eight months now; I've gone through every emotion imagin-able at least a hundred times each. I have accepted this reality, I'm just a lot more cautious now.

I see people differently after understanding my whole truth. It's not that I don't trust people at all. I do. But I also get kind of stuck on the concept and what it means. I trusted Mom, the one person who should have always had my back. I got burned badly.

Thinking through all the ways she let me down, I have come up with a long list of times she put me last. And it's not that I think I should always be top of the pile; it was a big family and she had a lot of responsibility. But she never did put me first. Not before Gene, not before Abraham. I was her child and I spent most of my life caring for her, not the other way around. I can see that now, and it's left a pretty big wound.

These days, when I ask someone the sort of question that prompts a personal response, I'll say, "You can answer honestly. There's no way possible you could ever hurt my feelings." I get odd looks, but people don't realize that my feelings are permanently broken. I don't know that they'll ever mend.

The nurse in me is saying, "Lori, these are all negatives." When I train nurses on writing reports and assessing problems, I always encourage them to note down positives and solutions as well as negatives. So, here goes: Mom was a lot like Keri. She was the family fix-it person. She gave calm reassurance to everybody she knew. A positive light in the world, she never had a bad thing to say about anyone. She loved her family, though the individual relationships . . . she needed a little work on.

It's now been a year since I bought that 23andMe kit. I can honestly say that it was the worst and best Christmas present I've ever given anyone. The worsts are easy to see. Finding out that I had no idea who I was brought up a lot of doubt. I was content to finish out my life thinking I was Gene's daughter.

The best part of finding out is being forced to deal with the demons I thought I had put to rest. My anxiety and feelings of isolation were there for a reason. I felt odd for a reason, not because anything was wrong with me. I also got to see how lucky I am to have Mark and Caitlen in my life.

Most of all, I realized that my voice has been missing from the world. Through my whole life, I have put my head down and just taken what's come. The abuse, the taunts of children, the social media chatter, all those voices talking at me and about me and no one ever heard directly *from* me.

This book is how I'm standing up for my truth. I have spent my whole life worrying about what people think. No more. I'm sharing my whole truth now, my veracity.

CHAPTER 14

The year 2020 began with me still struggling to figure out who I was. Some family were still unhappy with me, some were trying to figure out how best to support me, and with a biological father out there I hadn't met, I turned to the place that has always helped me find my voice: my work.

I'm so proud of the work I do. Looking back, my child-self did not expect to become a lifelong nurse, yet it makes so much sense given my childhood. At 19, I just started the nursing program thinking, "Well, I don't want to be a secretary, so I'll be a nurse." Those were literally the only options open to me at that time. Somewhere along the way, nursing turned from my job into my profession. Now, over two decades later, I've dedicated myself to being a servant to others, and especially to the patients I get to serve each day. It's a calling that I feel honored to be able to fulfill.

January

Early on in 2020, the healthcare industry was starting to hear reports about a new virus overseas that might be especially dangerous to our geriatric population if it reached the U.S. In February, a long-term nursing facility in Washington reported the first cases of an infection we were just learning was called COVID-19. Not

128 • LORI TUCKER

long after that, CDC guidelines came out to start wearing personal protective gear at all times; we started wearing masks, gowns, goggles, and gloves all day long.

It was a terrifying time because we knew so little about the disease and exactly how it spread or how to treat it effectively. Everyone who got it became deathly ill and died. So, prevention was our best defense, and we were all determined to keep it away from our residents. We were so lucky. All that spring there were no cases in our facility. It was a testament to our dedicated staff. Everybody was trying to do their best to keep our patients, ourselves, and our families safe.

March

Across the country, Americans had started to realize that COVID would be affecting everyone's daily life. By March, colleges and universities were starting to be concerned about having sick students on campus, especially in dorms with no one to care for them. Caitlen had transferred to the Miami campus of Johnson & Wales University, where the officials were watching the COVID crisis with great concern. Even though they had just resumed the semester after their spring break, it was decided that they were going to close the campus. All classes would be virtual for the rest of the semester and the dorms were closing. Out of nowhere, all students were notified that they had just three days to move out. Caitlen was so scared and so upset that she called me to try to figure out what to do.

"Mom! What is happening?"

"Come home, sweetie. You can do your classes from here," I said. While we spoke, I opened up my handy-dandy Southwest

Airlines app. It just so happened that there was a flight leaving St. Louis for Ft. Lauderdale (a Miami suburb) in a few hours for $97. What are the odds?

I called Mark at work, and he agreed to come home early so he could fly down and help Caitlen get home. He was on the next flight out within a few hours of the university's announcement being made. Meanwhile, Caitlen packed up and gathered what she would need to finish her semester from home. The two of them took turns driving Caitlen's car the 1,200 miles from Miami to Troy, Missouri. My girl was safely back by my side in 36 hours or so.

Walking in the door, she declared, "I'm staying in my room until this is all over!" Mark and I were glad to have her home but had no idea just how long widespread infections would go on.

Spring arrived in Missouri with its wash of green across the state that, unfortunately, residents weren't able to fully enjoy because we started seeing the first lockdowns. Assisted living and nursing homes were closed to visitors—including family members—effectively creating a little bubble of safety for all of us, though that made it really hard on residents. The nurses and doctors became the only contact for patients.

Staff were all issued ID cards with our names and occupations printed on them. Because the whole state was locked down for a period and no one was supposed to be traveling unnecessarily, we were supposed to show those cards if we were stopped by police and questioned about why we were out. I wasn't ever questioned, but one other nurse was. For a time, things seemed really dire . . . and they were.

June

As everything was locked down arguments started breaking out. Should we be forced to stay home and wear masks? What about our individual rights? I watched and saw something different from many others. I saw not just our dissimilarities, but the way that we were all one in this moment of communal siege.

Do you remember when the total eclipse happened a few years ago and, depending on where you were in the country, you could see "the ring"? A fraction of a moment seized in time for all of us to see the majestic blinding light that was revealed once the moon shifted past the sun. In that moment, people everywhere cheered.

That's what I think of when I think of COVID-19. Here was another brief period in our history where it didn't matter what color you were, or what political party you held your allegiance to. Everyone was so worried about each other: their families, their friends, and most of all themselves. COVID-19 brought us together as mankind because it was trying to destroy us all.

This flash of light only lasted a fraction of a moment. The delicate balance exploded in an instant. At the end of May, a terrible, unfortunate event happened in Minneapolis. A man named George Floyd lost his life, and all of America watched it happen. There were protests, even riots, across the country. Because we as a country were already on pause, there was nothing else to think about. Everyone was forced to consider this death and how it happened. As a woman of color, as a mother, and a nurse, I felt this unfortunate event deeply. I wasn't the only one. It drove a stake in the heart of all Americans—the entire world really. The dust has settled. Now is the time to heal for all of us.

As I have watched my country devolve into violence and arguments, I feel sad and frustrated at the lost opportunity. My wish for our country is to heal. It's OK to not all be the same. It's called diversity and we should celebrate our differences. Because we're all different, our country has stood the test of time for 244 years. We should celebrate a unity and togetherness that is born from our differences. We are the United States of America. The world is watching; let's lead the world through a celebration of life. One way to honor that life and those sacrifices is to wear a mask . . . for all of us.

July

Back at work, our little bubble remained COVID free. We felt fortunate, but worried that it was only a matter of time before we got our first case. Though I didn't think it was possible, it seemed like conditions at work got even scarier. I took full precautions, as did everyone on staff, washing my hands and sanitizing them until I had cracks on all my knuckles.

Then in July the inevitable happened. We started having positive cases. First it was just one patient, but then soon it was several. It spread quickly through our facility. Administrators created a hall that was only for COVID patients and the specific staff who worked with them. Only a few people were allowed to work in that hall, and I was one of them. We would be screened going in: temperature taken, answer the questions about symptoms, then we'd have to stay there for the rest of the shift—even on our breaks—to keep us from potentially spreading infection to anyone in the other parts of the building. I'd get to work in the morning and say a little prayer in the car before I entered the building every day, walking past the *Heroes Work Here* banner, feeling a strange mix of pride and fear.

For the first part of COVID, we wore goggles, masks, gowns, and gloves for every patient interaction and changed them between patient rooms. Sometimes as a nurse you need to hurry to a patient's side, but even if someone was struggling or needed to use the bathroom, we'd have to stand outside the door, hurrying into fresh gear before being able to do our jobs. It was horrible and scary, one of the worst things I've ever been through, and as you know, I've been through a lot.

One day, I was caring for a woman who had recently been diagnosed. She'd been so worried and so careful to avoid the virus. She just couldn't understand how she'd gotten this. As I was checking over her medications list, she began thinking out loud.

"How did I get this? Was it from the newspaper?"

She'd been getting the *St. Louis Post-Dispatch* delivered to her room each day. It wasn't from the paper. Unfortunately, it was inevitability that brought COVID-19 to our center.

I could tell from her eyes and demeanor that she was so mentally strong. But physically, this woman was not well—she was one of our sickest ones.

"I've had a wonderful life," she mused. She was so philosophical talking about all the good things she had experienced. It sounded to me like she was taking stock of her years. It made me teary.

Nurses can't keep six feet between them and patients, though we had been instructed not to touch the COVID-positive patients any more than necessary. As this woman talked to me, I reached over and held her hand. I probably shouldn't have touched her, but I didn't care. It was a touching moment and nursing isn't just about caring for the body.

She looked at my face and registered my sorrow. She patted my hand and said, "It's going to be OK." That just broke me.

I wasn't sick. She was. Here she was fighting for her life and *she* was comforting *me*.

I'm so happy to report that this woman whose grit saw her through over 80 years of life is still with us. She fully healed from her COVID experience.

It's times like that moment when I can see just how lucky I am to be working in a nursing home. As a nurse who has worked with geriatric patients for her whole career, I get to see what most people don't. When most people look at an older person, especially a very old person, they can't see past the wrinkles and gray hair. But when you take the time to sit down and talk with them, you realize that they have the same feelings that you do. They've experienced some of the same things. It's pretty special, actually. I get a window into the person that they are and can advocate for them.

The pandemic strained what was already a tough situation in my profession. We were all working extra shifts even before COVID due to a national nursing shortage. When caring for patients actually became life threatening, it got worse. Some nurses called it quits, mostly out of fear for their families. I understood not wanting to take that chance of being exposed or taking it home to a loved one. I wondered about it too, briefly. You can probably guess where I came down on that decision. We are nurses; we have to help the sick. It's our call of duty.

As a senior staff member who has worked at this facility for twenty-four years, I'm one of the leaders on the nursing team. I took it upon myself to help hold the team together. At the beginning of the COVID crisis, I started writing a short paragraph or two about our team members on the unit and sending it to our administrator. I felt it was important to always be positive and to call out certain nurses who went above and beyond every day to make our residents feel as good as possible. These great nurses are my comrades, my sisters, my friends; I applaud them all. Though every day was daunting, my work family really rose to the occasion.

One thing I always try to instill in new nurses is not to just look for the problems; the positives must also be recognized. You've got to figure out what works as well as what doesn't. Partly, that way of being has to do with me personally. I don't have a choice in keeping a positive mindset. I have found that dwelling on the negative points me down a bad psychological road. But the outlook also works well for me as a nurse because any problem that comes across my desk must have an answer. If I chart a concern, I make certain that I've also charted some resolution to that problem by the end of my shift, even if it's just notifying the physician. It's a mindset that has led to excellent outcomes for my patients over time, but it was especially important now, when every single detail mattered. Being a nurse in 2020 meant being on the front line of an invisible war.

I did my best to keep the illness from spreading at home. I can remember arriving home and stripping naked in the garage next to my vehicle. Wrapped only in a towel, I'd go straight to shower before greeting anyone in the house.

At work, we were all tested weekly for COVID, meaning a long swab all the way up the nasal passages. It was a little uncomfortable, as was wearing a mask all day every day, but it's what was necessary to protect our patients. This was just life in 2020; our health was watched closely every day.

The stress and long hours wore me out. I was feeling tired . . . exhausted really. I had developed headaches, weakness, and nausea. My back ached. I had also started coughing, and I was teary all the time. I wondered if it could be from wearing a mask so much. Part of me worried it might actually be COVID. I'd been caring for patients who had confirmed cases. My latest test was hung up in a lab somewhere. With thousands and thousands of people being tested, getting results was slow.

On July 26, I was just starting my day when my boss called me at home to tell me not to report to work. "I'm sorry, Lori, your COVID test was positive."

Crap.

I approached it calmly. I've been pretty whammoed since the age of five. I know how to weather a crisis. I took an inventory of myself. Breathing? Normal. Temperature? It was normal too (elevated temperatures were the only symptom I didn't get). I told myself, *I know I'm going to be OK.* People were recovering from this disease now; there was hope. And to be honest, I was already feeling better by the time I was diagnosed. It sickened me to think that I'd been contagious at work for a few days during the worst of my symptoms. Sadly, there was such a nursing shortage, there just wasn't anyone to cover if I had called in sick. I didn't want to leave one of my comrades on her own trying to cover an entire floor of COVID patients by herself. But now that there was laboratory proof of my illness, I was required to take two weeks in quarantine to rest and recover.

I realized we needed to have a family discussion. Mark and Caitlen joined me at the kitchen table to talk over what this diagnosis meant. One extremely contagious person in the household meant that everyone should stay away from me and should also stay home and not go to work or even the store.

"Do you want me to set up in a separate part of the house?" I asked.

"We're a family; we're in this together," they said. We quarantined immediately.

Mark's company brought him a computer and all the necessary equipment for him to work from home. He settled right in.

Over the next week, I continued feeling exhausted and had periods of pain. One day in the shower, I couldn't catch my breath at all and I had to sit down on the tile for about five minutes, trying to take air in and let it out. Luckily, though I was miserable, I was never in danger. I was able to be treated at home with just rest and

Tylenol if needed. I knew in my heart I was going to be one of the lucky ones; I was going to survive this illness!

As I was recuperating, I got a lot of well wishes and notes from fellow nurses who wanted to make sure I was OK. Even family members of patients I took care of checked in and sent their thoughts and prayers. I was so grateful for all their kindness. It made a difference.

On a day I felt well enough to talk on the phone for a bit, I called Jerry, my biological father.

"I have COVID," I said.

"I'm very sad today," he said.

I assured him I was feeling good, just fatigued for the most part.

Caitlen and I had originally planned to meet Jerry over the summer. We had a date all picked out to fly to Los Angeles to finally connect in person, but COVID restrictions kept keeping us apart. I'm so glad I didn't go. I wouldn't want to have possibly given him the virus. He's in his eighties now, and I was afraid of what that would mean for him. As of this date I've never met my biological father. Perhaps that's just the way it's supposed to be.

As I was healing, Mark started saying he wasn't feeling well. I checked his temperature. It was 101.4.

"Oh no!!!"

No mystery there, we knew what it was before any confirmation from a lab. It was COVID. We made contact with our family doctor who sent us to a testing site. By the time Mark arrived at the designated area, his temperature had reached 102.7. They swabbed him, he snorted a little and coughed. Sure enough, a few days later we got confirmation that he now had the virus too.

When Mark is sick, he gets really sick. A few years ago, he had pneumonia that almost killed him. So this diagnosis was scary; I was more concerned for him than I was for me.

Poor guy had very high fevers, mostly at night. Since I'm a nurse, I felt confident that we could do everything we needed for him at home and could avoid the hospital for all but the most dire situations. I remember lying in bed at night, Henry the German Shepherd between us, listening to Mark toss and turn, trying to find a cool spot to soothe his fevered body. His breathing was always steady, which comforted me. Tylenol took care of the rest.

For about a week he had intense fatigue. No more work Zooms for Mark. We were both lying around watching reruns of *Chopped* and trying to stay awake for a few hours at a time. Thankfully after ten days, the fevers and fatigue subsided. Mark had made a full recovery. Even better, Caitlen never did get a single symptom. If she had COVID, she was asymptomatic.

Fall

Though individual people have lost family members and dear friends, as a whole the numbers lost worldwide are hard to comprehend. Through the end of summer and all of the fall, everyone in my profession witnessed so much death. As a nurse in 2020, this experience has been like nothing anyone on earth has seen since 1918. Not since the influenza pandemic have this many people all died from one diabolical illness.

Now that a vaccine has been developed and is rolling out around the U.S., I feel like I've come through a crucible. And though I would never say I was lucky to have the experiences I did, part of my ability to see this storm through was because I was always in a storm from day one. As a survivor of childhood abuse, I faced COVID with some steel in my spine.

Finding out about the identity of my biological father seemed to symbolize that my life had come full circle. With all the things that have happened in my life, I've made the choice to be a survivor, not a victim of the bizarre occurrences. I know I'm not one in a million; probably half the world has been touched by abuse in some way. I just thought it was time to put a voice to this situation.

It was time to say, this happened to me. And because I shared it, I am stronger. The art of communication is paramount. Don't close yourself down. Connect. Connect with people who can help you. Connect with your veracity.

AUTHOR'S NOTE

Caitlen: I am your number one fan. I've always wanted you to have every opportunity to succeed. I love you, Caitlen, with all my heart. You are my everything.

Mark: To my husband, my partner, my love: our relationship has tested itself over and over, making us stronger each day. Our schedules are different, but our goals and strengths are the same.

To family and friends: I want to apologize to anyone I personally knew for being elusive or nonexistent as far as Facebook, Instagram, or Twitter is concerned. I'm not on the sites mostly because I'm a very quiet, shy person, but also my sister is always talking about someone being mad at someone for something they said on Facebook. I barely have enough time to be me, much less make someone else mad at me. I wouldn't want that anyway.

To my craft, nursing: I've had the great privilege of working for the same great nursing facility for over twenty-four years. I've had a long history there. While working for this company, I found out I was pregnant, I found out my mother had cancer, heard Abraham collapsed and died, and talked to my biological father Jerry for the first time ever. To say this company is my working family would be a huge understatement.

I'd like to thank my dear, dear friend Geniece Hughes for listening to me wonder out loud if *Veracity* should ever be written. She never wavered in her support. She is my colleague, my comrade, my friend.

To any man, woman, girl or boy that has experienced a similar situation to mine, my heart goes out to you. It's an unbearable pain that doesn't go away. If you need help or just want to put a voice to your madness, please tell someone. Anyone! Connect, connect, connect! You can find help in your family, your friends, or even your healthcare provider, if needed. If you're a child and you don't feel comfortable talking about it at home, tell your teacher, tell the parent of a friend, wave down a policeman. Don't let it be bottled up and become something you can't talk about. You are worth it. Your feelings do matter! It's OK to not be perfect; it's OK to say, "I'm hurt!" It's OK to ask for help if you need it, but it's not OK to feel that you don't have a voice.

To the O'Haras: Don, Dean, Laura, and Colleen. Thank you so much! Don made me feel so strong more than anyone will ever know. He was the reader; I was the writer. The entire O'Hara family made me feel safe while I was writing *Veracity*. This book couldn't, wouldn't, have been written without you. May God bless them and keep them forever.

To my doubters: For those of you who say, "Why the book?" I've always thought I had something to say, and I was always told it would be better not to say it. I finally got the courage to give myself a voice, to have my thoughts heard—not in an overbearing way, but just to say, "Enough is enough." These are my thoughts, my feelings, and for once in my life I felt like it was time to be heard.

About the Author

Lori lives in Lincoln County, Missouri and enjoys spending time with her daughter Caitlen, Husband Mark and their adorable pets Henry, trooper and Emmy. She has been writing for the past 18 years, VERACITY is her first published work. Lori believes becoming a survivor and not a victim is one of her best accomplishments.

Made in the USA
Monee, IL
28 February 2022

92011794R00090